T

Prophecy
Flow...

Apostle Michael P. Sterling

utix

UPON THIS ROCK, REVIVAL
OF THE FIVE-FOLD MINISTRY

UPON THIS ROCK, REVIVAL OF THE FIVE-FOLD MINISTRY

DR. MICHAEL P. STERLING

Library of Congress Control Number: 2013911360
ISBN: Hardcover   978-1-4836-5815-5
               Softcover   978-1-4836-5814-8
               Ebook   978-1-4836-5816-2

This book was printed in the United States of America.

Rev. date: 07/09/2013

To order additional copies of this book, contact:
Xlibris Corporation
1-888-795-4274
www.Xlibris.com
Orders@Xlibris.com
128547

CONTENTS

Dedication

This book is dedicated to The Church, The Body of Christ and those that long for the day that the church will come back into the unity of the faith, One Lord, One Faith, One Baptism.

Ephesians 5:27—That He might present it to Himself a glorious church, not having spot, or wrinkle, or any such thing; but that it should be holy and without blemish.

One Church

"Come Lord Jesus"

ACKNOWLEDGEMENTS

It is an honor to give thanks to GOD who gave me the golden opportunity to do this wonderful book on the FIVE-FOLD MINISTRY. I would like to express my gratitude to the following people who have helped me along the way. First and foremost, I give my sincere gratitude to my sister, partner, and friend Bishop Claudia Marshall. It is a hearty pleasure to thank Mama Bessie McDowell, who prayed me into the Kingdom and Gloria Hilton, who birthed me in, and the seed donor, who I never really knew. I would like to express my very great appreciation to my first born son, Jakuma Yasen, my eldest daughter, Leoshie Sterling (Mims), and, Malcolm Mims, her husband who has been more than a son to me. My sincere appreciation goes also to the son of my heart, Rascheed Sterling, his lovely wife and mother of my grandchildren, Tyesha Sterling. To Desirea and Brandon Sterling, and Alexander Sterling (Kai), I'm so proud of you and to my many grandchildren and my great-grandchildren I have not met yet. I extend a special double-portion blessing to my spiritual sons and daughters, this is your legacy.

I am especially grateful and my sincere thanks are extended to Deaconess Melody Hampton, who sowed the first seed toward this project.

I would like to express my very great appreciation to Apostle-in-Training, Jonathan Klemm, for his valuable and constructive suggestions during the editing of this book. His willingness to give his time so generously has been very much appreciated and my grateful thanks are also extended to Prophet Tina Klemm. I wish to acknowledge the help they provided and whose patience and love helped to make this project a reality. Finally, I wish to thank Int'l Evangelist Rene Pryor, KOG Ambassador, for her support and encouragement throughout the work on this book and her beautiful layout and cover design. Lastly, I offer my regards and blessings to all of those who supported me in any respect during the completion of the project.

Apostle Dr. Michael P Sterling

FOREWORD

By Dr. Paula Price

Apostle Michael P. Sterling demonstrates in "Upon This Rock, The Ministry of the Fivefold," the Lord's urgency to His future ministers. In the 21st century, every minister of the church must be enlightened and inspired by God's impending shift from the old to the new. All of us feel God's pressure to discover and implement a different way of doing church and kingdom. The revelation and prophecies contained in this book are a good response to that pressure. It reinforces the Lord's most pressing mandate upon His modern ministers, which is to flip church leadership right side up.

Clearly, the writer shows years of wisdom and close communion with the Holy Spirit in his presentation of the King of King's dictate on ministry of tomorrow; that is, the full reinstatement of apostles and prophets at the head of His church. Rich with scripture and practical experience, he points the way for up and coming apostles and prophets and propels the ministry of those poised for change. His words reignite apostolic fervor, redefines church leadership and governance, and realigns ministry leadership with its founder's vision—a vision of apostles partnering with prophets to move His church toward its eternal paths.

Using historical examples and modern relevance, and by grounding the work in what has been, advances the process. The apostle enables those reading his book to discern easily what Christianity will look like when God's people cease to fulfill their ministries and instead resolve to fulfill God's will. Joining the ranks of those undertaking the task of restoring the Lord's people and ecclesia to His dominion, Apostle Sterling lays down more tracks for the ultimate destiny of this and future kingdom generations; in a word, Christian living and kingdom service conformed to the founders of the New Testament church, the apostles.

The first apostles, being intimate eyewitnesses of the Lord Jesus Christ with the Apostle Paul, set forth the Lord's design of His church, articulated in Ephesians 4:11 and 1 Corinthians 12:28. Both names apostles and prophets as the first ministers of His church with the 1 Corinthians 12 reference expressly naming them hierarchically as first and second. The spirit and intent of both passages are caught and portrayed by the help minister and member of the Christian church prepare for what is to come. With wisdom and counsel he eases their concerns over the sweeping changes to affect Christ's church, using logos and rhema to motivate their cooperation with the apostles and prophets taking their place in kingdom service and Christian ministry now and in the future.

Bless Apostle Michael P. Sterling for his valuable contribution to the Lord's apostolic and prophetic reinstatement plan.

Dr. Paula A. Price

Chief Apostle, New Era Apostleship Restitution (N.E.A.R.)

Author of The Prophet's Dictionary and The Prophet's Handbook

President and Founder of Kingdom Embassy University

INTRODUCTION

Upon This Rock I will Build My Church

Jesus says in Matthew 16:18, "And I say also unto thee, that thou art Peter, and upon this rock I will build my church; and the gates of hell shall not prevail against it." It was this divine revelation of Jesus being the Christ (Messiah, Anointed One), Son of the Living God, which gave Peter access to the keys of the kingdom. It is by this same revelation that a young monk named Marin Luther would declare and understand that the just shall live by faith, thus beginning a reformation of the church.

This book is designed to continue the process of reformation, as in the 16th Century, where a partial reformation began to take place. Martin Luther, who we now realize was a prophet in his own right, was given a doctorate of theology at the University of Wittenberg (Germany) by the Electon Frederick, Duke of Saxony. This degree Staupitius was conferred upon him in October 19,

1512. This divine revelation caused him to speak boldly against certain indulgences, such as one could buy a soul from purgatory for ten shillings and not a farthing less. This indulgence was prefabricated in pretense by Pope Leo X, who succeeded after Julius II. This Pope Leo X imposed such ridiculous practices on the pretense of raising money for war against the Turks. Martin Luther began to oppose the Pope, much like a latter day Amos, who came to Bethel and heralded against King Jeroboam, King of Israel, and Amaziah, the Priest of Bethel. This prophet, Martin Luther, began the genesis of reformation. Martin Luther also was the first to translate the New Testament into the German language, which was September 1522. He studied the works of Desiderius Erasmus who prepared important new Latin and Greek editions of the New Testament. Martin Luther also finished the Pentateuch in 1523, thus completing the entire bible and publishing it in 1530. As we examine history we find that Martin Luther was a step ahead of William Tyndale. His great defiance was enacted as he nailed the 95th Thesis of Contention to the Wittenberg church door, as he declared his intolerance against the Roman Catholic corruption on Halloween night 1517. Martin Luther died of natural causes although he was branded a heretic by the Catholic Church. William Tyndale was not so lucky, and was burned at the stake in the public square (1596).

As we examine church history we see a clear picture of martyrdom. And in its wake men like John Wycliffe, who was called the morning star of the Reformation era, who 200 years prior criticized abuses and false teaching in the Catholic Church. Yes, John Wycliffe, a professor at Oxford University, was expelled from his teaching position by the Pope, who also after his death exhumed his bones and had them burned. This is the price of Reformation. Let us examine for a brief moment John Huss, using Foxes Book of Martyrs as our source. John Huss was chosen as the pastor of the Church of Bethlehem in Prague. He also held a position as the Dean of Students and Rector at the University. He along with John Wycliffe were known as the pre-reformers. His teaching and revelation upset the pope, and he was also burned at the stake like so many spirit filled saints of the time period. It is noted in historical data that John Huss was heard singing in the midst of the flames as he went on to glory.

Reformation and the Protested Movement

In the 15th Century the Protest movement led to the creation of the Protestant church, which came against ecclesiastical structure of the Roman Catholic Church. The Lutheran churches became popular in Germany, Switzerland, the Netherlands, and throughout Scandinavia. As this snowball began to roll down the hillside of revolution, it would endure many battles as the landscape of religious Babylon would forever be changed. In the midst of these transitional periods there would arise such great stalwarts as John Wesley, who along with his brother Charles, is credited with the foundation of the Methodist movement, which was highly successful throughout the United Kingdom and is now worldwide, from the Methodist Episcopal Church to the A.M.E (African Methodist Episcopal) and Richard Allen. John Wesley's 39 Articles of Anglicanism was adopted by the church in 1784. John Wesley's teachings were in great contrast to that of John Calvin, his predecessor (1509-1564) in the Reformation. John Calvin, whose Presbyterianism and church governance typified the rule of the Presbyters or ruling elders, believed in predestination and the unconditional election of man (justification by faith).

The Pentecostal Movement

On April 14, 1906, an African American preacher by the name of William J. Seymour started what is now known as the Azusa Street Revival in the city of Los Angeles, California. This one meeting continued almost nine years, where many of the

Orthodox churches came against this movement, which was characterized by the Baptism of the Holy Spirit and outbursts of speaking in tongues, signs, miracles and many wonders from this great movement that is now known as the Apostolic Faith Mission, which paved the way and influenced many of the Wesleyan Holiness denominations. William J. Seymour and the Azusa Street Revival became a springboard to the Church of God, COGIC, the Assemblies of God, and the Pentecostal Holiness Church. There are nearly 500 million Pentecostals across the world today. It's amazing to recognize God's Word becoming Rhema when he said he would use the foolish things of this world to confound the wise. We salute a half-blind preacher from Azusa Street, William J. Seymour.

The Charismatic Movement

In 1960 on Easter Sunday, Dennis Bennett, rector of St. Mark's Episcopal Church in Van Nuys, California, recounted his baptism in the Holy Spirit. This outpouring of the Holy Spirit caused a birthing of the Charismatic movement throughout many of the mainstream churches. The Baptism of the Holy Spirit with the evidence of speaking in tongues began to take place spontaneously as Acts 2 began to become rhema. The Catholics,

Protestants, and Episcopalians alike began to be affected by this snowball of change.

Let us now continue down this hill where some of the great fathers of the faith are now identified. Historically we see men like Smith Wigglesworth, known as the Apostle of Faith, who manifested God's word through miracles, signs, and wonders. This Pentecostal preacher's life and healing ministry touched and influenced women like Amy Simple McPherson (1890-1944), a well-known evangelist and founder of the Four-Square Church. To be also noted among the great American evangelists at this time was Billy Sunday, who was converted to Evangelical Christianity in 1880, and became a fire and brimstone preacher. He preached against the demon of alcohol and was a staunch supporter of the prohibition era. As we begin to examine some of the great teachers of our time, who were not the fire and brimstone evangelists of the past, but those prolific teachers of God's Word, we find men like Kenneth Hagin, Sr., Fred Price, Kenneth Copeland, Creflo Dollar, Jerry Seville, and many others who were influential in the Faith Movement. Even in the Charismatic circle, men like Benny Hinn, who saw women like the great Katherine Kuhlman, were all influenced by the Reformation.

These men protested and gave their lives to establish the Reformation and the Protestant Movement. The Protestant movement was established to correct the errors that were found in the Roman Catholic Church. One movement after another arose—and the process of reformation is not complete. The question is why? The answers are to be found written within the essence of this book. After looking over the historical data, now we can begin to understand the fragmentation of the church, where so many of our forefathers' works were undone. One revelation after another with divine understanding and enlightenment had to battle with hermeneutics, (which is taken from the Greek god Hermes, who was the god of gods), which is the art and science of interpretation, simply put logos not rhema.

Apostolic Wind Blowing Across the Nation and the World

From the Prophetic to the Apostolic Movement, divine order is the order of the day. First and foremost we must understand that the Prophet prepares the way for the restoration of the Apostle and the Apostolic Movement. From the time of Dr. Martin Luther King, a prophet of God, who was assigned to bring about a civil and humanitarian change in America and the world. This prophet of God, who is the embodiment of a Jeremiah 1:10 prophet, reminded America that it held in its archives a declaration of independence and a proclamation of emancipation. These ever growing truths had to be settled before America could live out the true meaning of its creed. This prophet, Dr. Martin Luther King, Jr. gave his life as a martyr, thus becoming one of this century's greatest pontificators. He rooted out segregation, he pulled down the sign of racism that said Whites Only, while helping to destroy a back-of-the-bus mentality. He thus threw down, or should I say laid down his life for America, his friend. In his last speech, I've Got a Dream, he began to prophecy a vision of brotherhood and the end of discrimination.

I say now to my bright brothers, who are leading this movement and caught in the wind of change, it is time to unite the church, the body of Christ, the kingdom of God.

To Peter Wagner, Chuck Pierce, Bill Hamon, John Eckhardt, Cindy Trimms, Paula Price, Dutch Sheets, Cindy Jacobs, and to the other apostolic and prophetic voices caught in the wind of change, beware of camping out at the revelation that God has given you. The cloud is still moving. David is coming out of the cave of Adullam. From obscurity these manifest sons of God shall arise. There is a changing of the guard. Let he who has an ear hear what the Spirit is saying to the church. Some of the names written above will be gone on to eternity to join the great pioneers of reformation like Oral Roberts, John Osteen, Bishop Earl Paulk, Benson Idahosha and many of the end-time generals.

Now, let's go back to the foundation and build the church from the blueprint and prepare a bride without spot of wrinkle for the second coming.

First we must begin to understand that in order to complete the process we must take a look at the very bedrock of its foundation. Any good builder knows that if the foundation is shaky, or is not established correctly, the building is suspect. You cannot remove a cornerstone or a foundational brick without weakening the building or causing it to collapse. By removing certain foundational stones in the formation of the church, such as the Apostle and Prophet, it has caused severe damage. The church will not be destroyed, because grace has been its mortar and God is not a man that He should lie. "Upon this rock I will build my church and the gates of hell shall not prevail against it." This is God's word, and it is settled in the heavens.

In Isaiah 60 the word of God tells us to, "Arise, shine; for Thy light is come, and the glory of the Lord is risen upon thee." This Light represents the truth, and the truth will set the church free and bring it back to the very foundation upon which it was first established. Ephesians 2:20, "And are built upon the foundation of the apostles and prophets, Jesus Christ himself being the chief corner stone," verse 21, "In whom all the building fitly framed together groweth unto an Holy Temple in the Lord."

The Prophetic and Apostolic Movement is to reestablish the Apostles and Prophets in the hierarchy of the Church, to undergird it, to oversee it, to establish it, and give it divine direction. The Church shall be a glorious house as we move back to the future.

The Fivefold Ministry or ascension gifts given unto the body of Christ are for the perfecting of the saints for the work of the ministry. The ascension gifts or the fivefold did not exist in totality until Jesus ascended up into the heavens. There were the Apostles of the Lamb who walked with Jesus. John, the Baptist, was the first dispensational prophet in the New Testament Era. But the ascension gifts of the Apostle, Prophet, Evangelist, Pastor and Teacher did not exist until Jesus had ascended. The Apostle Paul is noted among the first apostles, or "ascension apostles," to hear the Lord speak after His ascension. "Saul, Saul, why persecuteth thou me?" (Acts 9:4). He was also called out (ekklesia—the Church), and sent forth (Apostolos = Apostles). The word ascension is taken from Ephesians 4:8-11 where it says "He that descended is the same also that ascended up far above all heavens, that he might fill all things." We must understand that the fivefold ministry was not given to the body until Jesus Christ ascended upon high. That's when he gave gifts to men.

Once again I reiterate, the Apostles of the Lamb are those who walked with Jesus. The Ascension Apostles are those that have had a divine encounter with Jesus after He went up on high. That's how we coined the word "ascension."

Through this book you will begin to clearly see the fivefold ministry in full bloom, and begin to understand that the enemy has tried to disallow its existence through trickery, tradition, and religious persecutions. Let us now take a survey of the scattering of the church (Acts 8:1) from the time Stephen was killed and murdered and religious persecution began to take place on a grand scale. The church was exiled throughout the region and began to expand as great martyrs were sacrificed in the cause of Christ by the hundreds of thousands. This martyrdom continued until the time of Constantine the Great, who began to defeat the enemies of God by a noble sign of the cross and brought peace to the church for a thousand years. Whereas he set forth this general proclamation that no man was constrained to any religion but given liberty to all men to persist in their profession without any danger. After his death the power of the Pope and Bishop began to manifest the old adage as true; that is, absolute power corrupts absolutely. As the process of exalting the Apostle Peter above the rest of the apostles as a deity of sort, thus began the Papacy or the pope god/man. But as time moved on there arose an army of generals, men such as Martin Luther, John Wickliffe, and John Huss, who were also prophets of God in their own right, and Reformation had begun. Most of it started with Catholicism. The prophet Martin Luther began Reformation, we will complete the process.

In the book of Acts 2:34-35 the Word says, "For David is not ascended into the heavens; but he saith himself, the Lord said unto my Lord, Sit thou on my right hand, until I make thy foes thy footstool." God is waiting on you . . .

Ephesians 4:8, Wherefore he saith, when he ascended up on high, he lead captivity captive, and gave gifts unto men." (The Fivefold) . . . God is waiting on you . . .

Ephesians 4:10-11, "(He that descended is the same also that ascended up far above all heavens, that he might fill all things.) And he gave some apostles; and some prophets; and some evangelists; and some pastors and teachers." . . . God is waiting on you . . .

Hebrews 10:12-13, "But this man, after he had offered one sacrifice for sins forever, sat down on the right hand of God. From henceforth expecting till his enemies be made his footstool." God is waiting on you. Jesus is literally sitting on the bench waiting on the manifestation of the sons of God to run the ball. He is interceding and cheering us on. Wake up Zion! God is waiting on you.

There is a rumbling in the Church; a shaking that will cause everything that can be shaken to be shaken to the core, so that everything that cannot be shaken can remain. The church shall be triumphant and the latter glory shall be greater than the former. Zion will arise out of the ashes of days gone by. Out of the destruction, as monuments built unto men begin to fall, Zion will break forth like a tender blade of grass shooting up through cement and concrete floors. Through asphalt jungles this blade defies all matter and stretches forth its blade to touch the sun. So shall Zion stretch forth its mighty hand as prophesied in the book of Joel 2:1, "BLOW YE the trumpet in Zion, and sound an alarm in My holy mountain! Let all the inhabitants of the land tremble: For the day of the Lord cometh, for it is nigh at hand." Yes, the trumpet has sounded . . . Did you hear it? Verse 15 "Blow the trumpet in Zion, sanctify a fast, call a solemn assembly."

While Jesus sits on the right hand of God waiting for His enemies to become His footstool, Psalms 110:2 states the Lord shall send the rod of thy strength out of Zion (The Church), rule thou in the midst of thine enemies . . . It is the church that has been built up by the Fivefold Ministry which will bring the saints into one accord, who will do the greater works. Do you want to see the manifest glory (miracles, signs, and wonders)? Bring the apostles and prophets back together with the pastor, evangelist, and teacher for the perfecting of the saints. Yes, the very hand of God!

We can see it in shadow form as Moses' hand was lifted in Exodus 17:11. The Word of God says, "And it came to pass when Moses help up his hand, that Israel prevailed: And when he let down his hand, Amalek prevailed." The Amaleks smote Israel when they were weary and faint and had just come out of Egypt. So Aaron and Hur had to sit Moses on a stone (rock) symbolic of Christ. Exodus 17:12-13. Let's restore the Fivefold ministry and lift up the hand of God's chosen vessels that will be used to mold the Church into a church without spot, wrinkle, or blemish.

Jesus said, I do nothing unless I hear it from My Father (John 5:30). The Army of God must begin to move as a unit for full effectiveness. We are losing the war, because we are scattered by denominations, cultures, and race. We all have the same DNA, the DNA of Adam, and the blood of Jesus. We must come together in rank and file. Refer to Joel 22:7 . . . He prophesies about an army that will not break ranks.

The Fivefold must understand its Position [status], Rank [standing], and Authority [exousia] to be effective in this move of God. It has already started. Do you know your position? In the military of the good ole USA, everyone knows their position, operation, and assignments . . . We have different branches of the military—the Army, Navy, Air Force, Marines, National Guard, and the Special Forces, Navy Seals, Green Beret, the Rangers and a few others. They all move as one. In the Iraq war under President George H.W. Bush, for instance, everyone completed his or her assignment and victory was quick and decisive. That's what the church will be doing, as the withered hand becomes totally restored and functional. This book is designed to root out false doctrine, to pull down idolatry, to destroy Babylonian religion, to throw down monuments to men, and build the church not made with hands, but will flourish as a tree planted by rivers of water.

Jeremiah 1:10—Calling all Prophets!

We recently had a conference in the Inland Empire. The theme was Calling All Prophets. It is time for prophetic judgment to come into the church, to begin to root out, and to pull down, and to destroy, and to throw down, to build and to plant.

(Jeremiah 1:10) It is the Prophetic ministry that will come forth as the vanguard of God, crushing the Babylonian and Jezebel spirit of control, manipulation, and idolatry that has caused this downward spiral of the church. Yes! The prophets must begin to bring judgment into the house of God. The Church may once again rise up and live out the true meaning of its creed.

There have been many prolific expositions of God's word throughout the ages that have given great understanding and regulatory insight into the scriptures. God has used men like John Knox, John Calvin, John Wesley, and Charles Finney just to name a few. These men have become a vital part of this great reformation, and we must understand that God is forever unveiling himself. We must never remove the ancient or old landmarks, but this we do know, that is, to camp out is a cardinal sin. God is as the river and the wind and the rain; He is forever moving, immutable (without change), but forever manifesting Himself. Society could never at one time bear the full weight of His glory as Moses found out in Exodus 18:33.

I Peter 4:17, "For the time is come that judgment must begin at the House of God."

Apostle M.P. Sterling

Chapter 1

UPON THIS ROCK
THE MINISTRY OF THE FIVEFOLD

"And I say also unto thee, that thou art Peter, and upon this rock I will build my church; and the gates of hell shall not prevail against it." This foundational scripture, found in the book of Matthew, Chapter 16, verse 18, is a quote by our Lord and Savior Jesus Christ on the revelation that Peter had of him being the Christ. Upon this revelation the church was to be built, not upon the man Peter, as Catholicism sought to do—enthroning him as the first unofficial Pope. All authority is based upon revelation. "But who say ye that I am?" Peter acknowledges that He (Jesus) is the Messiah, the anointed one. This is the fulfillment of the prophecy found in Isaiah 7:14, Emmanuel, God with us; Isaiah 9:6, "Wonderful Counselor, the Mighty God, the Everlasting Father, the Prince of Peace." The Chief Cornerstone in I Peter 2:6 is also contained in the scripture, "Behold I lay in Zion a Chief

Cornerstone, elect, precious: and he that believeth on Him shall not be confounded."

Today's religious spirits, or the 21st Century Pharisees, are still stumbling at the Word CHRIST through their analytical theological dissertations or having attended the seminary of the frozen chosen. This is where those who have chosen ministerial hierarchy as a career goal are still eating the stale manna. The word clearly states in Hebrews 5:4, Let no man take this honor unto himself, but he that is called of God, as was Aaron. So there is a steady diet of Logos . . . with no Rhema; there is no light because there is no revelation. The word of God clearly states in Amos 3:7, "Surely the Lord God will do nothing (I repeat nothing), but He reveals His secrets unto His servants the prophets." This is an Old Testament precept, which cannot be changed, only enhanced. The enhancement is found in Ephesians 3:3-5, "how that by revelation He made known to me the mystery (as I have briefly written already, by which when you read, you may understand my knowledge in the mystery of Christ), which in other ages was not made known to the sons of men, as it has now been revealed by the Spirit to His holy apostles and prophets." Apostle Paul talks about the abundance of revelation that was given to him as he was caught up to the third heaven and heard unspeakable words, which it is not lawful for a man to utter.

You may ask, what is the point that this author is trying to convey? The point is stated in the epistle of James 1:17, "Every good gift and every perfect gift is from above, and cometh down from the father of lights, with whom is no variableness, neither shadow of turning." God is the same yesterday, today, and forever. His Word states that the Spirit reveals mysteries and revelations unto His holy apostles and prophets. For this is a foundational principal, a precept, a defining statement about revelation revealed unto holy apostles and prophets, and God has not changed.

In the book of Ephesians 2:19-21, "Now therefore ye are no more strangers and foreigners, but fellow citizens with the saints, and the household of God, and are built upon the foundation of the apostles and prophets." The foundation is primarily for governmental covering and oversight ministry, a spiritual covering so the word of God would be made manifest or revealed through these anointed gifts.

Jesus says, "Upon this rock I will build My Church and the gates of hell shall not prevail against it." Well, the gates of hell have divided the church and have stripped away the very foundation of the apostles and prophets by creating numerous denominations.

Abraham Lincoln, the 16th President of the United States, was faced with a crisis of monumental proportions. He saw a nation doomed to destruction; half slave, half free. The foundation of the nation was based upon life, liberty, and the pursuit of happiness. Yes, Freedom and Democracy! Even though our nation has not lived out the true meaning of its creed, it was a constitutional precept, which was enhanced by the Emancipation Proclamation. Even though we have strayed away from the Word of God and its foundational principles, it is not too late for the church to rise and shine.

We must get back to the basic principles of the Word. We must do it the Bible way. We must embrace the fivefold ministry. Yes, there will be charlatans, fakers, and frauds, "but alas there are several thousand that have not bowed their knee." There are many true apostles and prophets throughout the world, hidden in caves of obscurity awaiting "King Saul's demise," (Religious spirits or 21st Century Pharisees to fall or die). Some will seek to go on without the Prophet and commit spiritual suicide. It will be like going into the holy of holies without the mantle of the priest. Others will have their Damascus awakening. They will fall from their spiritual high horses, hear the voice of God, give up everything, and seek their Ananias (prophet) to receive sight and direction. Their ministry will be greater than ever before.

We are talking about the manifestation of the sons of God for whom the whole world is awaiting. The ozone layer is waiting for the revealing of kingdom sons, who clearly understand that the meek will inherit the earth. They will not sit idly by watching big business (Babylonian Empire) or consumer consumption (Babylonian lifestyle) destroy the very atmosphere we breathe in the name of the almighty dollar. I am talking about oil spills polluting our seas, the rain forest being systematically destroyed . . . the earth is groaning! Do you hear her?

Prophetic Decree . . . We declare and decree this Saturday (Sabbath) morning July 15, 2000, from Nigeria, West Africa, Auchi Edo State to the world, that there shall be an awakening, a stirring, and a shaking. Every Babylonian influence and every religious spirit shall be exposed. It shall be laid out naked in the face of the one true living God, Jesus the Christ, by the power of the Holy Ghost. We decree that the foundation of the church has already been laid. This is a now foundation; based on now apostles, now prophets, and a now Jesus.

Paul is dead, Silas is dead

Jesus is alive and has a remnant of Apostles and Prophets that have been hand selected, chosen and prepared for war. The weapons of their warfare are not carnal, but mighty through God to the pulling down of (denominational) strongholds.

Their revelation and knowledge of the Word of God will be so awesome and clear that the sheep will know that they have truly heard from God. Scriptures that we have been reading for years will become so illuminated and crystal clear. Just as in Luke 24:32, "And they said one to another, did not our heart burn within us, while he talked with us by the way, and while he opened (revealed) to us the scriptures?"

Upon The Rock of Revelation I Will Build My Church

The revelation of Jesus Christ, the Word made flesh, the revealing of His Word. "In the beginning was the Word and the Word was with God and the Word was God." Matthew 16:17, "And Jesus answered and said unto him, Blessed art thou, Simon Barjona: for flesh and blood hath not revealed it unto thee, but my father which is in heaven."

Authority is Based upon Revelation

Those with true spiritual authority that walk in the office of the apostle or prophet will be known by the revelatory knowledge of God's Word. We will witness in awe as the Word of God is revealed, where even a small child can understand

and apply it. In Amos 3:8, the prophet expounds on a time coming of spiritual destitution, where the Rhema word will be rare. There will be famine, not of bread nor of water, but of hearing the Rhema word of God. The preacher will preach Logos, but there will be no revelation. Jeremiah 23:21, "I have not sent those prophets, yet they ran: I have not spoken to them, yet they prophesied." These false prophets and apostles will continue to sell stale manna like modern day gurus who are destroying and scattering the sheep, promoting and upholding denominational madness. As religion continues, celestial palaces and monuments unto men will begin to fall. Great edifices of thousands will dwindle down to a few hundred. Chaos, that demon of destruction, will play a familiar song from times past as Nero begins virtuoso . . . but alas, "it is not over 'til it's over." (Quote: Yogi Berra, New York Yankees).

From the Caves of Obscurity

God's Generals will come like a refiner's fire, the manifest sons of God as prophesied in Joel Chapter 2. The word of God says a fire goeth before them, and behind them is desolation. They will come from the caves of obscurity—apostles linked with prophets being led by the Holy Spirit. They are the manifest sons of God. The prophet Joel describes them as a great army that will not break ranks. They will have such an anointing, a harmonic bliss, a synchonicity, a oneness, that will be unstoppable.

Surely ten thousand will be put to flight, as Enoch and Elijah's touch of agreement will cause nations to shake and principalities to crumble before the two golden lampstands which brings forth the golden oil (Zechariah 4). Their revelation of God's Word, properly understood and applied, will cause the great wealth transfer to take place. The wealth of the wicked will fall into the hands of the righteous. Our cup will run over with abundance, masters will become slaves overnight, and the last shall become first. This new wine will burst forth like insatiable rain upon a desert floor, turning desolation into an oasis. The marketplace apostle will go forth in kingdom power as the great wealth transfer begins to take place. Distribution of the king's wealth will begin to establish God's covenant as he swore to Abraham, the father of faith.

I Corinthians 4:20, "For the kingdom of God is not in word but it power." Luke 10:19, "I give unto you power to tread upon serpents and scorpions and over all the power of the enemy." When divine order comes back to the church, we will not have a residual anointing, but full measure to enable us to part the Red

Sea, to open blind eyes, to raise the dead, while opening and shutting the heavens at will.

The Revelation Anointing

An example would be when Joshua heard the instructions from God. He commanded the people not to speak while marching around Jericho for six days, and on the seventh day they shouted and the walls came tumbling down. It will be that simple. Psalms 110:3, "Thy people shall be willing in the day of thy power, in the beauties of holiness from the womb of the morning: thou hast the dew of thy youth."

And You Call Yourself an Apostle or Prophet

Amos 3:7, "Surely the Lord God will do nothing, but He revealeth His secret unto His servants the prophets." Show me your revelation: Show me some divine insight that you did not get from a book, seminar, a T.B.N. program or a cassette series. Show where God has revealed unto you the mysteries contained throughout the 66 sacred books. Tell me some of the new truths that have been hidden from the sons of men according to Ephesians 3:5, "Which in other ages was not made know unto the sons of men, as it is now revealed unto His holy apostles and prophets by the Spirit."

Show me how through prayer and meditation as a chosen vessel of God operating in the office of Apostle or Prophet what God has revealed unto you from the mysteries and secrets of His very heart. No, I am not from the state of Missouri, but show me anyhow. In Paul's conclusion to the church at Rome, he states in Romans 16:25-26, "Now to him that is of power to establish you according to my gospel, and the preaching of Jesus Christ, according to the revelation of the mystery, which was kept secret since the world began, But is now made manifest, and by the scriptures of the prophets, according to the commandment of the everlasting God, made known to all nations for the obedience of faith." Further reference is in Daniel 2:19, "Then was the secret revealed unto Daniel in a night vision. Then Daniel blessed the God of Heaven." Daniel as a prophet of God can be raised up in the enemy's camp because of the divine insight the office of the prophet holds. This is not something you can be taught at seminary, this is a sovereign anointing given by God, where he marks a vessel before the dawn of time, thus sealing him before conception.

Jeremiah 1:5, "Before I formed thee in the belly I knew thee; and before thou camest forth out of the womb I sanctified thee, and I ordained thee a prophet unto all nations." This cannot be bought, taught, or stolen. In this century the true prophets and apostles of fire will reveal many charlatans, fakers and frauds.

Have You Caught The Revelation? Upon This Rock I Will Build My Church.

No wonder Jesus prayed so hard in John 17:21, "That they all may be one; as thou, Father, art in me, and I in thee, that they also may be one in us: That the world may believe that thou hast sent me." No, not just a mere 120 souls, but millions of spirit-filled believers in Christ Jesus all in one accord. Talk about storming the gates of hell. Abortion will not stand a chance. Prayer reestablished in schools will be a minor task. Divorce American-style will be a thing of the past. For covenant agreement within the church will stand the test of time and eternity. Divine health will be ever prevalent throughout the body of Christ, as the blood cells of His divine church are rejuvenated one by the other. Example: the Elders will lay hands on the sick. They will immediately recover, for the oil will be thick, the dead will be raised by an anointed spoken word. The blind eyes will see by anointed spit being applied to the eyes. The apostles of God will send handkerchiefs all over the world.

They will be laid upon people oppressed by demons of cancer, AIDS, tuberculosis, yellow fever, and many other demons of hell that would try to raise its ugly head in the face of a unified church. Powerful prophets of God will call Christians out of whole cities before destruction hits. Famine will be widespread for the children of darkness, but the children of light will have no fear as they live in the abundance of the Word, truly understanding that man shall not live by bread alone, but by every word that proceeds out of the mouth of God. As the Prophets of God start to bless our meal barrels, they shall not wax empty. Matthew 10:41, "He that receiveth a prophet in the name of a prophet shall receive a prophet's reward." As these 21st Century prophets, anointed and appointed by God, come forth we will without hesitation give them our very last. "Behold our meal barrels shall not wax empty." The Word of God will no longer be something to look at and study for information about Christ. It will be our survival kit, our compass and guide that must be applied daily. As darkness covers the earth and gross darkness the people, we will arise and shine and the Gentiles shall come to our light (Gentiles=heathens, non-believers). We are spiritual Jews, no longer to be referred to as Gentiles. They will come saying, what must I do to be saved?

The Revelation of Jesus Christ

The Apostle John writes from the Isle of Patmos, Revelation 1:10-11, "I was in the spirit on the Lord's day, and heard behind me a great voice, as of a trumpet saying, I am the Alpha and Omega, the first and the last: And what thou seest, write in a book, and send it unto the seven churches which art in Asia; unto Ephesus, and unto Smyrna, and unto Pergamus, and unto Thyatira, and unto Sardis, and unto Philadelphia, and unto Laodecia."

This great Apostle John in the bleakness of life's challenge has been exiled to this island prison where he can no longer be a threat to established Judaism or religion, or compromise the security of Rome. For the great apostles of that time had turned the world, as they knew it, upside down.

The very bedrock of civilization stood on the fault line of truth, while the dudamis rector scale was measuring 6.66. Mankind as a whole had missed their time of visitation. The promised Messiah had arrived as a hermit clad in hippie clothes, profoundly declaring on this planet called earth, "I did not come to bring peace but a sword." He came to be an algebraic word or a mathematical equation that would begin to divide the wheat from tares, the dross from gold, and the church of Jesus Christ from the old religious order.

We must understand that historians believe that this Apostle of God had been boiled in oil, and it has been recorded that he swam during the whole process. John, who was now exiled to the island Patmos, begins to write about thrones, judgments, powers, principalities, and things past, present, and things to come. He writes about seven seals, seven trumpets, and seven plagues. He writes about the last days in metaphors and parables that are illusive to the novice, and total Greek to the non-believer.

It seems as if Steven Spielberg or Alfred Hitchcock could have written some of the scenes that John beheld; being caught up in the spirit on the Lord's Day. But the Word of God says only those who have an eye to see will see, and only those that have an ear to hear will hear what the Spirit is saying to the church. John in his darkest hour, when all humane normality had ceased, where the cruel and bitter treatment was not even befitting an animal—in the midst of all this, John does not complain. In the first chapter and the ninth verse, he states emphatically that he was in the spirit on the Lord's Day. 99.9 % of today's Christians cannot remain in the spirit through a traffic jam; we are so full of the flesh, so selfish, and so confused, that if Jesus came, he would not recognize us as His disciples. Why does this condition exist within the so-called church? The false prophets have diluted and polluted God's Word, sending the church in the wrong direction. John, the revelator, writes the epitaph to the seven churches as a final letter of warning—to repent or else they will lose their candlestick. This letter, the book we call Revelation, was given to a man, who had truly been separated and consecrated before the Lord, to repair the breaches that exist, even more so today as we speak. For the seven churches spoken of here represent the church as a whole, number seven equals a completed church. He writes in his expose that the church has left her first love. He also writes about those who claim to be (spiritual Jews) are of the Synagogue of Satan. Also, they have allowed the doctrine of Balaam to enter the church, the doctrine of the Nicolaitans. The Jezebel spirit is attempting to subdue the church; this is what exists today within the church. Let's examine the Jezebel spirit in today's church.

The Jezebel Spirit

The Jezebel spirit is one of power, influence, manipulation, and control. As we examine Jezebel, the wife of Ahab, king of Israel, we must look closely at who Ahab was. In I Kings 16:29-33, "And in the thirty and eighth year of Asa, King of Judah, began Ahab, the son of Omri, to reign over Israel: And Ahab the son of

Omri reigned over Israel in Samaria twenty and two years. And Ahab, the son of Omri, did evil in the sight of the Lord above all that were before him. And it came to pass, as if it had been a light thing for him to walk in the sins of Jeroboam, the son of Nebat, that he took to wife Jezebel, the daughter of Ethbaal king of the Zidonians, and went and served Baal, and worshipped him. And he reared up an altar for Baal, and worshipped him. And he reared up an altar for Baal in the house of Baal, which he had built in Samaria. And Ahab made a grove; and Ahab did more to provoke the Lord God of Israel to anger than all the kings of Israel that were before him." This Ahab, King of Israel, was said to have been more evil than all the kings of Israel before him. His choice to take a pagan wife, Jezebel, would ultimately lead to the destruction of herself and her husband. Ahab was indeed a mighty warrior who married this Zidonite woman, whose beauty and charm inevitably lead to Israel's departure from Jehovah God to the worship of Baal. This spirit of manipulation and control is prevalent throughout many of today's churches; even more so in this prophetic age, as the Jezebel prophets prophesy more about fancy cars and houses than being an oracle of God.

We seem to forget Jehovah-Jireh is our provider. These things are retroactive for the seed of Abraham. Note this Jezebel spirit would change the direction of the vision God has for the local assembly or the church universal. The Jezebel spirit is never in the seat of authority, but she sits very close. This enables him or her to weave a tangled web that ultimately destroys the vision, the visionary, and even Jezebel herself. This tantrum-throwing, false accusing, propha-lying, manipulative and controlling spirit will slip into your choir, board meeting, or even the pulpit itself to stop, delay, or hinder the plan of God. It has caused division in the church universal through self-grandeur and having the audacity to think you're the only one receiving revelation from God. Listen, my friend, you must understand that Jezebel will pump you up, tickle your fancy, and even blow smoke in your eyes while telling you it's the Shekinah Glory. It will have you so full of yourself, if you are not careful, you'll find yourself sitting in the midst of 40 false prophets dressed in the latest royal apparel. They will be speaking swelling words that will tantalize your soul, soothe your emotions, and sugarcoat your frailties. And when God's true prophet shows up in an old suit and speaks Ebonics, you'll miss the very move of God.

It is imperative that we begin to challenge the false prophets, behead them, and usher in the new order. Man or woman of God, the journey is too long for you alone. God has appointed and anointed an Elisha to walk out the latter end of this journey with you. As you begin to mentor him, he will leave his natural father, mother, and all family values for a day in the sun. The light and glory of the mantle that you are carrying sometimes can be seen by everyone except you. Whether you happen to be on Mount Carmel executing the false prophets of God or running in fear of Jezebel's tyrannical power or hiding in a cave wishing to die, you are still God's chosen vessel. It is imperative that you raise up spiritual sons to carry on the mission.

In the book of Malachi Chapter 4 verse 5, the word of God says, "Behold I will send you Elijah the prophet before the coming of the great and dreadful day of the Lord. And he shall turn the hearts of the fathers to the children, and the heart of the children to their fathers, lest I come and smite the earth with a curse." Upon this rock, I will build my church and the gates of hell will not prevail against it.

It is the Elisha army of prophets and fivefold ministry that will carry the double portion of anointing that can only come from one who has served under a seasoned fivefold gift with their whole heart. In Malachi 4:6 it says I will turn the heart of children to their fathers. It is most definitely a matter of the heart, those who recognize the Christ anointing in the life of their mentors (fathers in the Lord). As a Peter when asked, who do you say that I am? This army of sons will carry a patriarchal anointing and blessing that will be summoned by kings and governmental authorities of this day. As we enter into the culmination of the Ages, where darkness is covering the earth and gross darkness the people, these (Elisha) sons will arise and shine as beacons of light in a lost and dying world. The Jehoshaphat of today when besieged on every side will cry out! Is there a prophet of the Lord that we may inquire of him? The answer will come; there is a fivefold ministry gift that has served under the mentorship and tutelage of a great man or woman of God, (who has poured water on the hands of Elijah). This is why Malachi is saying I will smite the earth with a curse, if this does not happen. Jesus himself left twelve sons to carry out his mission; how many sons are you training up to carry on the vision? Are you leaving them a great heritage and legacy to follow? Or do you have a castration mentality; killing the very prodigy that God has sent to carry on after you have finished your course?

In ministry today I know from personal experience that men, who are supposed to be fathers, may become jealous and even afraid of their spiritual sons' anointing. Many times the Saul spirit rises up and tries to kill the anointed David that has been called to be the successor. You cannot kill David. He will march from the cave of Abdullah (obscurity) with his mighty men of valor and be ushered into the kingdom. He is not a threat to anyone but the kingdom of darkness. As a son he will minister to you as you head toward glory, passing the mantle onto your modern day Elisha. As this governmental transition begins to take place, your Hazael and Jehu will show up as a new order begins to take place.

Chapter 2

THE APOSTOLIC CLOUD
And
PROPHETIC FIRE

The Burning Bush or the Prophetic Fire is seen in the book of Exodus 3:2, where the word of God says, "And the angel of the Lord appeared unto him in a flame of fire out of the midst of a burning bush: and he looked, and behold the bush burned with fire, and the bush was not consumed." As we move forward let us examine bible history where the omnipotent God manifested as prophetic fire. Clearly God becomes the Prophet of Fire who calls Moses aside to see this phenomenon of the bush that burns with fire without being consumed. Now the prophetic finger of God speaks from the midst of the fire, commanding him to take off his shoes, for he was standing on Holy ground. Thus, the consecration takes place, and Moses is given a divine mandate, to bring Israel out of Egypt. Thus God appeared in the midst of the fire to birth a deliverer.

This same (Manifestation of God, Prophet of Fire) shall be seen all through Israel's journey across the wilderness. In the fire by night with revelatory insight this New Testament number two in the Fivefold must point direction in the midst of the darkness when we cannot see our way. We must call for the seer who can peer through the darkness of confusion.

Example: when King Jehoshaphat was going into a great battle, this mighty king asked, "Is there a prophet of the Lord that we may inquire of him?" The answer was: There is Elisha who poured water out on the hands of Elijah. They called for Elisha, who was separated as a prophet by the chariot of fire. We must follow this example. As Apostles, Prophets, Evangelists, Pastors and Teachers, when things get confusing and we realize our steps are crucial, critical, yet uncertain, we must inquire of the prophet who will give us divine direction. When the body of Christ starts to function as an organism we will avoid many of the hardships, failures, and pitfalls that occur much too often in ministry.

While in Nigeria, West Africa I was conducting a lecture at the Living Gospel Outreach Bible College. I asked one of the young pastors to assist me in an exercise. I asked him to hold a bottle of Evian water in his left hand. I then grabbed ahold of his index finger and asked him to remove the cap from the bottle; he tried furiously with no success. I then released the index finger and grabbed hold of the thumb; again it became impossible. The experiment was to show him how the body of Christ has lost its power because the Fivefold ministry was not functioning together. It further showed then that without the thumb, the apostle, the hand of the Fivefold ministry has little or no power at all. Without the prophet, it loses over half its strength. But with the apostle and prophet together the cap is removed quite easily. There is no stronghold that can withstand this powerful anointed team.

The Cloud by Day and Fire by Night

Exodus 40:38, "For the cloud of the Lord was upon the tabernacle by day, and fire was on it by night, in the sight of all the house of Israel, throughout all their journeys." There was an Apostolic cloud and a Prophetic fire. The tabernacle is a shadow of the foundational church. For the Ark of the Covenant was set within the tabernacle. Ephesians 2:19-20, "Now therefore ye are no more strangers and foreigners, but fellow citizens with the saints, and the household of God . . . verse 20 . . . And are built upon the foundation of the apostles (cloud) and prophets (fire), Jesus Christ himself being the chief cornerstone." Jesus Christ is represented as the Ark of the Covenant within the tabernacle or the temple. I Corinthians 3:16 says, Do you not know that you are the temple, (tabernacle) of God, and the Spirit of God dwells in you? The cloud by day is a representation of the apostolic covering of God, which appears throughout the book of Exodus, descending upon the mount and then as the tabernacle is completed. This apostolic presence of God becomes a covering descending and ascending. When it descends, everything remains still as the glory of God is revealed in different manifestations. In the wilderness journey our omnipotent God becomes Jehovah-Jireh: As the children of Israel began to complain, the "I am God" supplied manna in the wilderness.

Let us examine Exodus 16:18 with Acts 4:35. In the book of Acts the apostle became a distributor unto every man according as he had need. In Exodus the supply of manna was given as every man had need. Exodus 16:18, "When they did mete it with an Omer, he that gathered much had nothing over, and he that gathered little had no lack: they gathered every man according to his eating." So the "I AM GOD" cloud by day becomes an apostolic supply. So the nation is once again satisfied for a while, and God's man Moses continues to follow the cloud by day, thus leading a chosen nation onto the promise land. But alas, this rag-tag nation will murmur and complain throughout their journey, and their dead bodies shall be scattered on the desert floor bleached and scorched by doubt and unbelief. At times they are ready to stone their deliverer Moses and return to the bondage of Egypt: Are we so different? Shall we neglect so great a salvation and fall after the same example of unbelief? We have God's compass and guide for our journey through the wilderness of preparation. There are 66 books contained in our Holy Bible. How can you allow yourself to fall into the same pit?

Hebrews 3:1-2, "Wherefore holy brethren, partakers of the heavenly calling, consider the Apostle and High Priest of our profession, Christ Jesus; Who was faithful to him that appointed him, as also was Moses in all his house." Are you faithful to him who has brought you out of Egypt? Are you faithful to him who is leading you through your wilderness journey? Or, maybe you are gathering stones to throw at your 21st Century Apostle, your modern day cloud by day, who is God's representation of covering, protection and supply? Hebrews 13:17, "Obey them that have the rule over you, and submit yourselves: For they watch for your souls, as they that must give account, that they may do it with joy and not with grief: for that is unprofitable for you."

Let Me Prophesy For a Minute. "For death and life are in the power of the tongue." This Apostle of God will not allow the people of God to anger him as they did Moses to the point of seeing the promise land and unable to enter. I am speaking about an earth manifestation, the Kingdom of God, a little bit of heaven here on earth. We are truly the lender and not the borrower, above and not beneath. The wealth of the wicked has been released to the righteous. Divine health is the norm. As Satan is truly put under our feet, whole cities are set free as we cast down the demonic forces that have been assigned to different regions. I declare and decree that we are going over—with or without you. We will see you when you get there. Whether you are a father, mother, sister or brother, husband or wife, we shall enter into the rest of God. We shall claim our mountain; we shall march to our spiritual Hebron. We shall not break rank. We shall possess the land. We will rule with Him and we shall reign as Kings and Priests . . . in Jesus name, Amen.

Apostolic Cloud

The Apostolic cloud was seen by King David. Psalm 91:1, "He that dwelleth in the secret place of the most high shall abide under the shadow of the Almighty." David talks about a constant dwelling place, never to come from under this divine protection, under the shadow, under the cloud, under the Word or the apostolic mantle, where God has set his divine order. I

Corinthians 4:15, "For though ye have ten thousand instructors in Christ, yet have ye not many fathers; For in Christ Jesus I have begotten you through the gospel."

The Apostolic Father has set such a divine leading by the Holy Spirit, it would behoove you to follow as if following Jesus himself. Some of us get stuck on the man. We forget the office to which he was called. We forget the Word, and can be heard spouting phrases such as "Does God only talk to Moses?" In Ephesians 3:3 the Apostle Paul states, "How that by revelation he made known unto me the mystery," verse 5, "which in other ages was not make known unto the sons of men, as it is now revealed unto His apostles and prophets by the Spirit." God has not changed. His Word is steadfast. He just added the apostle to the equation. As we examine the Old Testament truth realized in Amos 3:7, "Surely the Lord God will do nothing, but he revealeth His secrets unto His servants the prophets." This has become a foundational truth bringing together the Old Testament with the New.

The Apostle and the Prophet become the Governmental Shoulders of Christ.

We can further explore this in the book of Isaiah 9:6, "For unto us a child is born, unto us a son is given, and the government shall be upon His shoulders and His name shall be called Wonderful Counselor, the Mighty God, the Everlasting Father, the Prince of Peace." God has always been around, as a covering Father. He wants to manifest Christ in you the hope of glory, not a paraplegic body that cannot respond to the signals from the head. If God's Word says that He reveals secrets to the prophets, and His revelations are make known to His holy apostles and prophets, then that settles that. It's the Word; stop trying to use your hermeneutic approach to it. Just apply it. The Word works!

The body of Christ has been ill, deformed long enough. It's time for divine order. When Jesus walked the earth he tried to give us prophetic insight into what he was looking for. Matthew 8:20, "Foxes have holes, and the birds of the air have nests but the Son of Man hath nowhere to lay His head." He came to line up a body even then, a body that would receive signals from the head, the chief cornerstone, and be led by the Spirit, thus becoming the body of Christ, the fullness of the godhead bodily. When one of the disciples asked him to go and bury his father, Jesus said follow me, let the dead bury the dead. He was grooming a body that would understand its priority, a kingdom that would hear His voice, understand His divine order, and follow. The Word of God says in Luke 18:29-30, "And He said unto them, Verily I say unto you, There is no man that hath left house, or parents, or brethren, or wife or children, for the kingdom of God's sake, Who shall not receive manifold more in this present time and in the world to come life everlasting." This is for the remnant, the elect, the few that are willing to sacrifice all for the kingdom. Not every believer can do this. Ask the rich young ruler.

As the fullness of the Godhead bodily, you are complete in Him, who is the head of all principality and power, Colossians 2:9-10. When we begin to understand that Jesus is coming back for a fully functioning body that is lined up in one accord, Jesus, the Son of man, will not lay his head on a non-functioning, out of order, confused body that does not even know if they should be Baptist or Presbyterian, Methodist, Pentecostal, C.O.G.I.C., Assembly of God, Lutheran, or Nazarene, or any other demon-nation, which is short for denomination (divided-nation). Even us who know the truth, are so careful to say, Well, let's not throw the baby out with the bath water. Well in the name of Jesus it's no longer a baby, it's a religious brat that is stopping the flow of the body coming together.

It is an anti-Christ spirit. We must understand that Christ is not Jesus' last name. It is the empowerment of the Holy Spirit, which rests, rules, and resides in the believer. Christ in you is the hope of glory. We must begin to understand that when anyone speaks against another member or segment of this multi-member corporate body of Christ, they cause division and sectarianism. Through denominational traditions and doctrines, the rudiments of men take on and become the anti-Christ spirit. It is imperative that we stop the division within the church and begin to come together as one, not divided by the many components that separate us through operations and administrations, but center on our love, belief, and commitment to Jesus, the Christ, who is the center of our faith.

I was watching a video last year where Dr. Mark Hanby was speaking at the Full Gospel Baptist Convention. Bishop Paul Morton was there, Bishop Eddie Long, a few hundred clergy, and thousands of Saints. Dr. Hanby said that he was glad that they received the Baptism of Fire, but they still cannot put new wine in old wine skins. You should have seen the look on some of the old guard. It took a lot of courage for the Tennessee white man to say that to all those black brothers. I love Dr. Hanby for that. He is truly a bright brother shining with the revelation of truth. We cannot continue to try and put new wine into old wineskins. It cannot contain the fermentation of the power. There is a new fermentation as I speak, and the old wineskin denominations cannot contain it. So throw the baby out with the bath water and let's have revival! God is not going to pour out the fullness of this latter rain until we come back to the foundational principles of HIS CHURCH. A sovereign God has set some in the church FIRST Apostles, SECONDARILY Prophets, THIRDLY teachers, and after the formula is complete, then Miracles.

Divine Order

I Corinthians 12:28, "And God hath set some in the church first apostles, secondarily prophets, thirdly teachers, after that miracles, then gifts of healings, helps, governments, and diversities of tongues. Let us examine the words, firstly, secondarily, and thirdly.

First—(Strong's Concordance)
Greek = proton . . . In time, place, order of importance, before, at the beginning, chiefly, the first of all.
First—(Webster's Dictionary)
Being before all others, with respect to time, order, rank, or importance.

Secondarily—(Strong's)
Greek = Dyoo'tenos . . . second, in time, place, or rank, afterward.

Secondarily—(Webster's)

Second after the first in place, time or value, next after the first in rank.

Thirdly—(Strong's)

Greek = tree'tos . . . order of a third part

Thirdly—(Webster's)

Next after the second in rank or decree, third place.

We understand in the Fivefold Ministry there is no preeminence/ superiority, but there is a divine order and formula for miracles, as we begin to exegete I Corinthians 12:28. First of all we must understand that it means exactly what it says. Number one, God has done this, (God hath set divine order in the church). An omniscient, omnipotent, God's word says He set first in the church Apostles. (Reflect just for a moment). If you were the Prince of Darkness, knowing your time was short and you were at war with the Kingdom of God being manifested in the earth realm through the church, what better way to cause confusion and disarm the church than by eradicating or eliminating the very office that He set in the church first, before all others, with respect for time, order, rank, or importance? Divine order is the call of the day! To set things in motion and prepare for the second coming, we must do it God's way. Remember when God told Moses in Exodus 25:40, "And look that thou make them after their pattern, which was shewed thee in the mount." This is type and shadow of God's immutability. When He says this is how it should be done, he means it. I do not mean to be redundant, but this point is essential. To understand the metaphor of cloud by day, you must begin to see it in apostolic terms. It was the cloud that moved by day that caused all Israel to break camp and follow. Those that failed to move died in the wilderness. God's divine order—Cloud by day; Fire by night. First Apostles, (Apostolic Cloud). Secondarily, Prophets (Prophetic Fire.) This team link up with Master Teacher produces Miracles. God set in the church first Apostles, secondarily Prophets, thirdly Teachers, after that miracles, then gifts of healing, helps, governments, diversities of tongues.

FORMULA FOR MIRACLES

Apostle + Prophet + Teacher = Miracles

Chapter 3

THE FIVEFOLD MINISTRY
APOSTLES

The Fivefold Ministry is as the withered hand in Luke 6:6-10 that has been drawn up, non-functional. The scribes and Pharisees (religious spirits) are still watching with indignation. But Christ will restore a healthy functional Fivefold Ministry. The Fivefold, or the hand of God, represents the very hand of Christ Jesus in the Church. You must understand that when He ascended upon high He gave gifts unto men (Ephesians 4:11). The very essence of who He was became available to the Church. He walked in all five gifts as the Apostle and High Priest of the Melchizedek order. In Hebrews 3:1, "Wherefore, holy brethren, partakers of the heavenly calling consider the Apostle and High Priest of our profession, Christ Jesus," Jesus is the Chief Apostle and architect of the Church, the spiritual Church, not the building made with hands, but the temple. According to I Corinthians 3:16, "Know ye not that ye are the temple of God, and that the

Spirit of God dwelleth in you?" When our Apostle and High Priest talk about the Comforter, He is talking metaphorically about Himself, who was all spirit in the first place as God (Elohim).

John 1:1, "In the beginning was the Word, and the Word was with God and the Word was God." Verse 14, "And the Word was make flesh, and dwelt among us, (and we beheld His glory, the glory as of the only begotten of the Father,) full of grace and truth." Yes! This Jesus gave us power to become sons of God, some to hold office in the Fivefold Ministry as an Apostle, Prophet, Evangelist, Pastor, or Teacher. Now there are some that claim to walk in all five. I beg to differ with you. Jesus walked in all five in fullness as the Godhead bodily, but no one else will manifest all five gifts. The Holy Spirit may give you grace as the need arises to function in the other gifts out of necessity, but set your ego down and consider Jesus Christ, the Apostle and High Priest of our Profession. He has blessed you to function in the fivefold, so excel in the one that's dominant, and let grace activate the others as the need arises. I am an Apostle and walk in a powerful Prophetic Anointing. I started out as an evangelist, I have been a pastor and I have taught at several Bible Institutes and schools of Theology, but first and foremost I am an ascension Apostle.

The Fivefold Ministry did not even start until the day of Pentecost. See Acts 2:1, 16; Joel 2:28. Before this supernatural endowment there were only the Apostles of the Lamb, the disciples, and the believers. The church began its progression on the day of Pentecosst. As the Church was coming into being, God was molding a young man at the feet of one of the greatest teachers of Judaism of his time, Gamaliel, who mentored Saul.

This young man was Paul of Tarsus, Saul, who would become one of the greatest Apostles of all time. He never claimed to be a pastor. No, he was a Father. I Corinthians 4:15, "For though ye have ten thousand instructors in Christ, yet have ye not many fathers, for in Christ Jesus I have begotten you through the gospel. Saul/Paul never claimed to be a Bishop nor a Pastor. He was an Apostle, a foundation layer to the New Testament Church. I Corinthians 3:10, "According to the grace of God that was given unto me as a wise master builder, I have laid the foundation and another buildeth thereon. But let every man take heed how he buildeth thereupon." Paul gave us warning that we need to be very careful in building upon the foundation that has already been laid. The brick mason's know that when you lay a foundation for a skyscraper you need to follow the blueprint of the architectural design.

Throughout each Pauline Epistle, the design of this great Apostle begins to take form. For instance, Apostle Paul begins to set Divine Order in the Church, as well as in the body. I

Corinthians 12 is full of his divine wisdom as he states in verse 12, "For as the body is one, and hath many members, and all the members of that one body, being many, are one body: so also is Christ." We must begin to understand that we are the body of Christ. Anyone who tries to stop the body of Christ from coming together has the spirit of the anti-Christ. Ephesians 4:3, says "Endeavoring to keep the unity of the Spirit in the bond of peace." The word "endeavoring" means to do everything possible to keep unity in the bond of peace. We do not have to do things the same way. Apostle Paul makes it clear. I Corinthians 12:5-6. "And there are differences of administration, but the same Lord, And there are diversities of operations, but it's the same God, which worketh all in all." We do not have to do it the same way. We can operate differently. It's okay, we can administrate our ministries differently, and it's okay.

I Corinthians 12:28 gives us rank and file in the Church. There is structure and theocratic hierarchy. Even though we are servants and are subject to the Holy Spirit as He moves, we are to be in tune and turned to the right frequency. For my sheep hear my voice. So when the Spirit speaks through a layman, novice, or even a child, we all submit to the Spirit. Only those who have an ear will hear. It is incumbent on the 21st Century Apostles to hear and obey when God uses any vessel. Maybe

He will use another "donkey" or an ass to get your ATTENTION. Let's explore I Corinthians 12:28, "And God hath set some in the church, first apostles, secondarily prophets, thirdly teachers, after that miracles, then gifts of healings, helps, governments, diversities of tongues." The Word "first" translated in the Greek is proton, which means first in time and place, rank in order of importance, at the beginning, chiefly, the first of all. Yes, simply stated first means first. Let's do it the Bible way, i.e. line upon line and precept upon precept. This mathematical equation just might work. If we can get the apostle + the prophet + the teacher = miracles. There is something about this formula that intrigues me. Miracles, healings helps governments, diversities of tongues, helps = pastor, ministers, and evangelists. Governments = bishops and elders. The church here was in divine order, because God set some in the church first, I reiterate, God set some in the church first, apostle. I still do not mean to be redundant, but faith comes by hearing and hearing and hearing.

Food for thought

It is very interesting that the word "apostle," apostles, and apostleship appears almost a hundred times in the New Testament, while the word "pastor" appears only once. It is quite evident that something is wrong with this picture. The word "pastor" appears in plural form in Ephesians 4:11, "and some pastors." If the bible is our source and reference, then why is the pastor, who we see all over the world and in churches everywhere, only mentioned once in the New Testament, while the apostle is mentioned 86 times? We have nothing against pastor in the fivefold ministry; it is our purest intent to provoke you to receive the restoration of the apostle and prophet ministry. The two brothers have come home with a foundation-laying mission.

In the book of Malachi 4:5-6 the Word of God says, "Behold, I will send you Elijah the prophet before the great and dreadful day of the Lord. And he shall turn the heart of the fathers to the children and the heart of the children back to the fathers, lest I come and smite the earth with a curse." God is saying through the Prophet Malachi restoration or else. The spirit of Elijah is a fathering spirit that brings about the patriarchal blessing . . . and a double portion to the obedient son. It solidifies the servant ministry through obedience. God is a God of divine order. Jehoshaphat said in II Kings 3:11, "Is there not a prophet of the Lord, that we may inquire of the Lord by him? And one of the king of Israel's servants answered and said, Here is Elijah the son of Shaphat, which poured water on the hands of Elijah."

This was the Chief Prophet's credentials; he had paid the price to receive the double portion blessing. This double portion or patriarchal blessing can only come from a father to a son; this is what Malachi 4:5-6 is saying. "Behold I will send you Elijah the prophet before the coming of the great and dreadful day of the Lord: And he shall turn the heart of the fathers to the children, and the heart of the children to their fathers, lest I come and smite the earth with a curse." It is those last few words which intrigues me the most. Here one is called to take responsibility for a bastard generation, and the other is called to submit, for submission entitles one to the double portion. I remember talking to my spiritual father, the late Apostle Joseph Sims, that it is better to be the son than the father. **Let he who has an ear, hear.**

Scripture Reference to the Word "Apostle"

I Corinthians 3:10. Acts 1:2; 2:42-47; 4:32-35. Galatians 1:19. Hebrews 3:1.
Ephesians 2:19-20; 3:3-5; 4:11.

The Apostle and High Priest Christ Jesus left a rich heritage and legacy to those who he had chosen to be apostles. Today's apostle will be endowed with supernatural power and ability and will change the very nature and course of the church, which we have known. You will not recognize tomorrow's church. It will come together line upon line and precept upon precept as the old cobblestones of tradition are uprooted (Bishop—Pope hierarchy), and the apostolic stones of the Apostle ministry are set in place with the Prophetic stones of the Prophets ministry, and they line up with the chief cornerstone, Jesus Christ Himself. Ephesians 2:21-22, "In whom all the building fitly framed together groweth unto an holy temple in the Lord; In whom ye also are builded together for an habitation of God through the Spirit." And I Peter 2:5, "Ye also, as lively stones, are built up a spiritual house, an holy priesthood, to offer up spiritual sacrifices, acceptable to God by Jesus Christ." This is the bible way. This is the foundation of the house that God built, the church of the firstborn, one Unified Universal Church. The word of God says, unless the Lord builds the house, they labor in vain that builds it: This foundation stone of the Apostles ministry will revolutionize the churches. It will no longer be concerned with a separate denomination, but the church as a whole as its top priority. This New Jerusalem Church will be glorious as it comes together in one accord. This one accord-ness is mandatory, so that God's presence and glory may once again fill the Tabernacle in fullness. The Apostle has a very lonely and difficult job ahead, but it is imperative that we, the saints of God, who have been waiting, travailing and interceding begin to support the ministry of the Apostle by laying our finances at the Apostles' feet as they did in Acts 4:33-35. Verse 33 says, "And with great power gave the apostles witness of the resurrection of the Lord Jesus: and great grace was upon them all. Neither was there any among them that lacked: for as many as were possessors of lands or houses sold them, and brought the prices of the things that were sold, And laid them down at the apostles' feet: and distribution was made unto every man according as he had need." (This is a commonwealth principle). As on the day of Pentecost when the Apostles Peter, James, and John were in the hierarchy of the church and were with one accord. The Greek work (Homothoomadon) Strong's #3661, Being unanimous, having mutual consent, being in agreement, having group unity, having one mind and purpose. The Apostles along with the disciples had an intellectual unanimity, an emotional rapport, and volitional agreement in the newly founded church. Homothoomadon shows a harmony leading to action. The word of God says in Acts 2:12, "And when the day of Pentecost was fully come, they were all with one accord in one place. And suddenly!

I, Michael Paul Sterling, declare and decree we shall come back together united as one church, one body of believers, and we will experience once again suddenly! I declare a spiritual awakening, a revolution through prayer, prophecy, and praise. I declare, decree, and call the church back into divine order. As an apostle of God I cast down every anti-Christ spirit that has caused division in the Church of Jesus Christ. I speak with the power and authority of Christ in me the hope of glory, come Forth, in Jesus name, manifest sons of God.

Beyond the Twelve

I think the most ludicrous teaching in Christendom is that the apostles were only those who walked with Jesus before his death, burial, and resurrection. Well in Acts 9 there was a young man named called Saul of Tarsus, who had a divine encounter with the Lord Jesus. Jesus explained to him that it is hard to kick against the pricks, Acts 9:5. And I say today in the 21st Century, it is still hard to kick against the pricks. God is going to have His way. Either you come down off your high horse of that religious spirit, or you will be thrown down as a Saul of Tarsus. There are literally thousands of legitimate apostles that God has hand selected and molded with His own hand in caves of obscurity, awaiting the sounding of the trumpet.

Other Ascension Apostles scriptural references

Saul = Paul—Acts 13:9, Romans 11:13, I Corinthians 4:9, 9:2.

Barnabus—Acts 14:14.

Andronicus and Junia—Romans 16:7 . . . these two are believed to have been chosen with the 70 that went forth.

Apollos—I Corinthians 4:6-9.

Epaphroditus—Philippians 2:25.

James, the Lord's brother—Galatians 1:19.

Notable = of note (Webster's = eminent)—high in station, rank or repute, distinguished, greatness, lofty, high prominent.

Apostolic Foundation

I Corinthians 12:28, "And God has set some in the church, first Apostles." The Apostolic covering becomes a father to the prophet, the evangelist, the pastor and teacher, and to the whole ministry at hand. The Apostle Paul states in I Corinthians 4:15, "For though ye have ten thousand instructors in Christ, ye have not many fathers in Christ Jesus." I have begotten you through the Gospel. This Apostolic Father has such a divine leading by the Holy Spirit, would it not behoove you to follow as if following Jesus himself? Some of us get stuck on the man and his personality. We cannot see or understand, he is God's chosen vessel equipped with a special grace to carry out God's mandate. Let us not be caught spouting such phrases such as, "Does God only talk to Moses?" The true apostle has revolutionary insight, and if you pay close attention, you'll find that he has become in many instances an oracle of God. In Ephesians 3:3 the Apostle Paul states, "How by revelation he made known unto me the mystery . . ." Also in verse 5 he further states, "Which in other ages was not made known unto the sons of men, as it is now revealed unto his holy apostles and prophets by the Spirit." God has not changed. His word is steadfast. He just added the apostle to the equation of that Old Testament truth in Amos 3:7, "Surely the Lord God will do nothing, but he revealeth his secrets unto his servants the prophets." This is a foundational truth bringing together the Old Testament with the New Testament. This foundational team is the bedrock of the church, which is divinely connected to the Chief Cornerstone of Ephesians 4:20.

In the book of Psalms, the Prophet David says in his 133 Psalm, "Behold how good and pleasant it is for brethren to dwell together in unity." David realized that when everything is in God's divine order that there is an anointing, a flow of God's power running down from headship, down the beard, saturating the entire body. When he begins to describe it as the dew of Hermon and Mount Zion, he speaks of an awesome power flowing downward, gaining force and momentum. That is the glory and power of God. The blessing is commanded by God. Think for a moment . . . a commanded blessing by God, just for dwelling together in unity! This is Apostolic and Prophetic, the pattern which has been ordained from before the foundations of the earth. In Revelation 21 the Apostle John wrote from the Isle of Patmos, He saw a new heaven and a new earth. He saw New Jerusalem coming down from heaven prepared as a bride for her husband. John further states in verses 12, "And had a wall great and high, and had twelve gates, and at the gates twelve angels, and names written thereon, which are the names of the twelve tribes of the children of Israel." Verse 14, "And the wall of the city had twelve foundations, and in them the names of the twelve apostles of the Lamb.

APOSTLES

Let's examine the word "apostle," its biblical root, definition, and function, so that there will be clarity of thought when the ministry of the apostles comes to mind. In the book of Luke 6:13 the Bible says, "And when it was day he called unto him his disciples: and of them He chose twelve, whom were also named apostles.

Apostles . . . Greek—one being sent forth for a specific purpose or commissioned to accomplish a specific task. The end-time apostle must be a builder, commissioner, ambassador, commander, church planter, foundation layer, general strategist, and a territorial warrior.

Matthias—chosen as an apostle. Acts 1:23-26. Verse 26, "and they gave forth their lots; and the lot fell upon Matthias; and he was numbered with the eleven apostles."

Saul = Paul—Separated and called to the Apostolic Ministry. Romans 11:13 . . . I Corinthians 4:9 . . . I Corinthians 9:2 . . . Acts 13:2-4. Verse 2, "As they ministered to the Lord, and fasted, the Holy Ghost said, separate me Barnabas and Saul for the work whereunto I have called them." Saul/Paul: Name changed Acts 13:9, "Then Saul (who also is called Paul,) filled with the Holy Ghost, set his eyes on him." Paul writes in Romans 11:13, "For I speak to you Gentiles, inasmuch as I am the Apostle of the

Gentiles, I magnify mine office." Paul writes in I Corinthians 4:9, "I think that God hath set forth us the Apostles last, as it were appointed to death; for we are made a spectacle unto the world, and to angels, and to men."

The Apostles called gods

As the supernatural power begins to unfold at Lystria, the man with the impotent feet begins to walk (Acts 14:8-15). Let's examine this great humility. As Barnabas and Paul begin to rent their clothes, telling the people it is not us, but the supernatural power of God you see at work today.

As the Ascension Apostles begin to be identified they will arise and shine forth the glory of God with an anointing and power unprecedented in today's church. Yes, these hand-picked generals will come forth from the caves of obscurity like a David, whose time is overdue. Their assignment is to prepare the body of Christ for the second coming, or the bride for the groom.

As we look over the books of II Corinthians, Acts, Galatians, and Ephesians we see further assignments and developments of the ascension apostles; that is, their care of the church, being chosen, their revelation of God's Word, the koinonia, and breaking of bread, the selling of property to support the movement, and the new apostolic order. We must understand the fellowship of breaking bread from house to house. This koinonia brought forth such an intimacy in the apostolic community as the church began to experience a common wealth.

Apostle

The Apostle is one of the Fivefold Ministries of Ephesians 4:11. It is a foundation-laying ministry (Eph. 2:20) that is seen in the New Testament by establishing new churches (Paul's missionary journeys), by correcting error, by establishing proper order and structure (I Corinthians), also acting as an oversight ministry that fathers other ministries (I Cor. 4:15, II Corinthians 11:28). Some major characteristics are great patience, and manifestations of signs, wonders, and miracles. We will know more and see greater manifestations concerning the apostle during the peak of the apostolic movement.

Acts of the Apostles

Acts 1:2, Ephesians 4:11, Acts 2:42-47, Acts 4:32-35

Acts 1:2, "Until the day in which he was taken up, after that he through the Holy Ghost had given commandments unto the apostles whom he had chosen."

Galatians 1:19, "But other of the apostles saw I none, save James, the Lord's brother."

Ephesians 2:20, "And are built upon the foundation of the apostles and prophets, Jesus Christ himself being the chief cornerstone."

Ephesians 3:3-5, "How that by revelation he made known unto me the mystery;" (as I wrote afore in a few words, whereby, when ye read, ye may understand my knowledge in the mystery of Christ), Which in other ages was not made known unto the sons of men, as it is now revealed unto his holy apostles and prophets by the Spirit."

Ephesians 4:11, "And he gave some apostles; and some prophets; and some evangelists; and some, pastors and teachers."

Acts 2:42-47, "And they continued steadfastly in the apostles doctrine and fellowship, and in breaking of bread, and in prayers."

43. And fear came upon every soul; and many wonders and signs were done by the apostles.

44. And all that believed were together, and had all things in common.

45. And sold their possessions and goods, and parted them to all men, as every man had need.

46. And they continued daily with one accord in the temple, and breaking bread from house to house, did eat their meat with gladness and singleness of heart.

47. Praising God, and having favour with all the people. And the Lord added to the church daily such as should be saved."

Acts 4:32-35, "And the multitude of them that believed were of one heart and of one soul: neither said any of them that ought of the things which he possessed was his own; but they had all things common.

33. And with great power gave the apostles witness of the resurrection of the Lord Jesus: and great grace was upon them all.

34. Neither was there any among them that lacked: for as many as were possessors of lands or houses sold them, and brought the prices of the things that were sold,

35. And laid them down at the apostles' feet: and distribution was made unto every man according as he had need."

In the last few verses, especially verses 34 and 35, we find that the saints have been so initiated by the Holy Ghost and resurrection power that they begin to sell land and houses in support of the ministry. Not only do they begin to sell their possessions, but also they bring the prices of the things that were sold and laid them down at the apostles' feet! Now faith in action causes the very hand of God to move even greater. To sell your possessions and lay the money at a man's feet, an apostle of God, you must have mountain-moving faith. This is another reason the church was so powerful, because they trusted the God in man, this deposit of the gift of Apostleship given unto certain individuals who began to impact the church like never before. There was such an anointing, where the glory of God became so evident that the shadow of one, an apostle called Peter, began to heal the people. This resident anointing was so great that two believers lost their lives because they lied in the presence of this glorious anointing, where the Holy Ghost was in full authority, Acts 5:1-10.

It is very important that we begin again to do ministry this way, a proven formula from God. Now there are many charlatans and fakers out there, but if you are led by the Spirit of Christ you will never go wrong.

As an Ascension Apostle I have traveled all across the country setting up prophetic seminars and teaching on the fivefold ministry. I have reset the governmental order throughout St. Louis, Cape Gerardo, Missouri, Sandusky, Ohio; Rochester and Harlem, New York; Columbus, Georgia; Arizona, California, Texas; South Carolina; Detroit, Chicago; the Netherlands, India, Mexico, and many parts of Africa. We have launched Schools of the Prophets and have empowered the saints with the knowledge that God is not satisfied with just one Benny Hinn or one Morris Cerullo, or one Oral Roberts, or how about just one Billy Graham? What about one T.D. Jakes? Listen closely! When Jesus ascended up on high he came back in the personification of the Spirit to empower a body of believers to walk in the totality of himself, with full authority. I quote, "Behold, I give you power to tread on serpents and scorpions, and over all the power of the enemy: and nothing shall by any means hurt you." (Luke 10:19). Now for you Bible scholars who wish to exegete this further, go to the book of Colossians, Chapter 1, verse 27, "To whom God would make known what is the riches of the glory of this mystery among the Gentiles; which is Christ in you, the hope of glory." And II Corinthians 4:7, "But we have this treasure in earthen vessels, that the excellency of the power may be of God, and not of us."

It is this Apostle's assignment to walk in the first person and destroy the spirit of the Nicolaitanes, which separates, controls, and holds power, thus separating the clergy from the laity. Let us understand that there is a separation, but not to the point of holding power to the point of self-aggrandizement or a utopian authority. We must understand the Bible says in Ephesians 4 that he gave some apostles, and some prophets, and some evangelists, and some pastors and teachers for the **perfecting of the saints** for the work of the ministry. The assignment is to activate Romans 1:11 where the Apostle Paul writes, "I long to see you, that I might impart unto you some spiritual gift, to the end ye may be **established**. The word established means: 1) to bring into being on a firm or stable basis. 2) to install or settle in a position. 3) to enact, appoint, or ordain for permanence. 4) to make a church, national or state institution. Now I come to establish you, the believer, as a wise master builder to be assembled and to be fitly framed together for a habitation of God through the Spirit. As an end-time contractor the apostleship ministry is designed to touch each believer as well as the other fivefold team. It is our job also to discern the levels of the gifting and the call of God on your life. Though you have ten thousand instructors, coaches, and mentors, yet you have not many fathers. In the book of Malachi Chapter 4 verse 6 let us pay attention to the last ten words, "lest I come and smite the earth with a curse." What this verse says is the heart of spiritual and natural sons is not turned to fathers, and the heart of spiritual and natural fathers are not turned to spiritual and natural sons, that their individual earth, not the world, will be smote with a curse. The reason for this prophetic declaration from Malachi, the prophet, in the last book of the Old Testament, minor prophets, before 400 years of silence began, this prophet Malachi declared as an oracle of God that sons and daughters would need a double portion anointing that only an Elijah father could bring to an Elisha son who would receive his mantle, thus obtaining the generational blessings that would be handed down according to the pattern of Abraham, Isaac, and Jacob, who produced Israel, the nation. I reiterate Malachi 4:5-6 says, "Behold, I will send you Elijah the prophet before the coming of the great and dreadful day of the Lord: And he shall turn the heart of the fathers to the children, and the heart of the children to their fathers, lest I come and smite the earth with a curse." It is in the generational blessing and heritage that God's word is fulfilled. Satan, the serpent, broke the natural progression through rebellious children. And there are now a generation of bastards in the earth realm. If and when these fatherless children return to God and receive Jesus Christ as their Lord and Savior and humble themselves under a spiritual father, they will receive the double portion anointing that is necessary for this end-time warfare. Faith comes by hearing and hearing, I reiterate, faith comes by hearing until you get it.

This apostleship office comes with an ambassadorship from the kingdom of heaven and its King Jesus Christ with full ambassadorial authority, as a sovereign in a foreign nation acts on behalf of the sending nation, power, or kingdom. The apostleship ministry is an eagle-eye ministry that comes into new territories and identifies the gatekeepers, while yet soaring up into the high places with spiritual authority dethroning principalities, powers, and rulers of darkness. This territorial warrior is equipped to do the job. The Apostle Paul states in II Corinthians 10:2-5, "But I beseech you, that I may not be bold when I am present with that confidence, wherewith I think to be bold against some, which think of us as if we walked according to the flesh. For though we walk in the flesh, we do not war after the flesh: (For the weapons of our warfare are not carnal, but mighty through God to the pulling down of strong holds;) Casting down imaginations, and every high thing that exalteth itself against the knowledge of God, and bringing into captivity every thought to the obedience of Christ." Now the next verse is real apostleship ministry. I announce and pronounce to Satan and all rebellion, we serve you notice, verse 6, "And having in a readiness to revenge all disobedience, when your obedience is fulfilled." I want to send out a clarion call, so blow the trumpet in Zion and sound the alarm in God's holy mountain for the day of the Lord is nigh at hand. I want the world to know that this is what's coming through men of God who walk in holiness and consecration. They will be the battle ax of the Lord and a sharp two-edged sword. Fire will proceed out of their mouths. This is a Joel army accompanied by the remnant and the elect. They are those who will not break rank. The word of God says this army has never been seen in the world before and shall never be seen again, for this is the final call. Let he who has an ear, hear what the Spirit is saying.

Prophetic Reflection

I, Michael Paul Sterling, can remember being at an International Prophetic Conference in Acapulco, Mexico under the authority of my spiritual father, Apostle Joseph Sims, (now deceased.) of End time Ministries. I was over the International Conference of ETM, and was assigned to speak on a Friday night.

I chose to speak on this topic, When the Prophet Turns Around, which was taken from II Kings 2:24, where the newly acclaimed prophet Elisha turned and cursed the four children who mocked him, and there came two bears out of the woods and "tare forty and two children of them." What I was ministering on, was that one day the prophet would no longer give you only a prophetic blessing, but as a battle ax of the Lord also bring judgment to all rebellion (Smile). This did not go over well at the conference, but it is the truth anyway. Examine the two witnesses in Revelation 11:3-7. Oh, by the way, Prophet Michael C. Monroe was with me at the conference and was set to speak on Saturday evening. It was in the month of May, 2003, he stole the show (for the gainsayer, he was on point). We're coming out of the cave. Get ready for the final chapter. Yes, it will be the manifest sons of God who the whole world is waiting on. Some prophetic time tables may be off, but it will surely come to pass. Read Romans 8:19-20; read it for yourself. I am not going to explain everything. Please read it.

The Apostleship Ministry

When we begin to evaluate the apostleship ministry and its downfalls, we must first begin to understand that Jesus was the first apostle of the New Testament Church, who chose twelve apostles, who are known as the Apostles of the Lamb. When he ascended up on high he gave some to be apostles, some to be prophets, some to be evangelists, and some to be pastors and teachers. He also spoke to a young Pharisee by the name of Saul, who would become Paul, while knocking him off his high horse. He is the embodiment of an Ascension Apostle. This apostleship ministry is serious business. Many are called, but only a few have been chosen. There are those that wear the title, but do not walk in the divine office of the Apostle. This ambassadorial office that is given by our Lord and Savior Jesus Christ is confirmed by seasoned apostles and prophets, who will lay hands on those that are chosen in the earth realm. First of all, a bishop cannot install an apostle. This is a critical error in church theology and will cause a ground swell of debate. But we will deal with that apologetically at another time. A bishop can be part of the ecclesiastical body or the presbyters, but he alone does not have the authority to lay hands and impart the anointing necessary to establish an apostleship ministry. Romans 1:11, II Corinthians 12:28, Ephesian 2:19-20. The Apostle Paul imparts spiritual gifts and is a part of the foundation of the church along with the prophet. As an apostle he is a seasoned presbyter of the Jerusalem council, where James, the Lord Jesus' brother sits in the chief seat and declares his Krino (sentence) with all due diligence concerning the Antioch question on circumcision. See Acts 15 where the apostles and elders came together to deal with the issue of circumcision.

In the Apostle Paul's letter to the Philippians, written while he was imprisoned in Rome, he addresses the saints, the bishops, and deacons at Philippi at Macedonia. These are those who are now overseers of the ministry which Paul founded on his second missionary journey. These bishops, elders, and saints are all under the apostleship of Paul.

Chapter 4

THE FIVEFOLD MINISTRY PROPHETS

The Index finger or the pointing finger represents the Prophets, which points direction. Without these two, the prophet and the apostle, there is little or no power at all. This is why the church is scattered in so many directions, because the apostle holds the fist together in a tight bond and the Prophet supplies the knuckle of power that sends the enemy to the floor. The word "prophet" is mentioned 71 times in the New Testament in singular form, and a total of 159 times in one form or another.

One of the divine commissions of the Prophet or prophetic movement is to point the way to the full restoration of Christ's Holy Apostles. As the prophet John the Baptist begins the inauguration process through which the apostle and high priest of the church, Christ Jesus, will come, this prophet, as an oracle of God, is the door by which the church will begin. It is incumbent that the first apostle, Christ Jesus, comes through the prophet John. For the word of God says in Amos 3:7, "Surely the Lord God will do nothing unless He reveals His secrets unto His servants the prophets." John becomes an eternal witness, as a voice that cried out in the wilderness, who now proclaims and witnesses the inauguration of the church age. He sees the Spirit descend on Him as a dove, and hears a voice from heaven declaring, This is my beloved son, in whom I am well pleased. Let him who has an eye see, and him that has an ear hear. The restoration of apostles is no threat or intimidation to the prophets, for they are to make ready a people to receive the ministry of the apostles. There will be no competition between God's true prophets and His new breed and generation of apostles. These two foundational stones of the church, the prophet and apostle, will launch the prophetic and apostolic movement as the apostle and prophet come together as a team understanding their metrons (measure of rule) of authority. There is no preeminence, they understand their rank and position and begin to flow together as the New Testament church begins to take form. The prophet and apostle will begin to co-labor and network together to fulfill their mutual ministry of preparing the kingdom sons for the next move of God, which is presently called the Manifestation of the Sons of God.

PROPHETS . . . The specialty of Prophets is their God-given ability to speak for God, not just to teach and preach the bible truths about God and His son, Jesus Christ. They have the special calling to speak "thus saith the Lord." The Prophet has a certain dimension of authority in his prophesying that others do not have. Those with the gift of prophecy, or those who function on the saints' level of prophetic ministry have the ministry of exhortation, edification and comfort. (I Cor. 14:3) Those who are truly commissioned prophets have the right to prophesy direction, correction, guidance, and new revelation to a kingdom, person, church, or nation. Some are used to pronounce God's judgments and reveal the calling and purposes of God to whomsoever God wants to personally express His thoughts, purposes, and specific will.

He is a man of God to whom Christ has given the ascension gift of a "prophet" (Eph. 4:11; I Cor. 12:28, 14:29; Acts 11:27, 13:1). A Prophet is one of the Fivefold ascension gift ministers, who is an extension of Christ's ministry to the church. He is an anointed minister who has the gifted ability to perceive and speak the specific mind of Christ to individuals, churches, businesses, and nations. Greek: prophetess (prof-ay-tis) a foreteller, an inspired speaker, (Strong's concordance, p. 62; Vine's concordance, p.894) A proclaimer of a divine message, denoted among the Greeks as an interpreter of the oracles of gods. In the Septuagint it is in the translation of the word "roeh" a seer, indicating that the prophet was one who had immediate intercourse with God (I Samuel 9:9). It also translates the word "rabbi" meaning "one in whom the message from God springs forth, or one whom anything is secretly communicated." (Amos 3:7, Ephesians 3:5).

Scriptural Reference

Amos 3:7, "Surely the Lord God will do nothing, but he revealeth his secret unto his servants the prophets."

Acts 15:32, "And Judas and Silas, being prophets also themselves, exhorted the brethren with many words, and confirmed them."

I Corinthians 14:29, "Let the prophets speak two or three, and let the other judge."

I Corinthians 14:32, "And the spirits of the prophets are subject to the prophets."

Acts 11:27, "And in these days came prophets from Jerusalem to Antioch."

Acts 13:1, "Now there were in the church that was at Antioch certain prophets and teachers; as Barnabas, and Simeon that was called Niger, and Lucius of Cyrene, and Manaen, which had been brought up with Herod the tetrarch, and Saul."

I Samuel 9:9, "(Beforetime in Israel, when a man went to enquire of God, thus he spake, Come, and let us go to the seer: for he that is now called a Prophet was beforetime called a Seer.)"

Amos 7:12, "Also Amaziah said unto Amos, O thou seer, go flee thee away into the land of Judah, and there eat bread, and prophesy there."

Isaiah 43:19, "Behold, I will do a new thing; now it shall spring forth; shall ye not know it? I will even make a way in the wilderness, and rivers in the desert."

The Prophet Jeremiah

Author: Jeremiah

Date: 616-585 B.C.

Theme: The prophecy of Jeremiah might be considered the great book of backsliding and the dangers of apostasy. Apart from this there is only one other book that mentions backsliding. (Hosea 4:16, 11:7, 14:4). Jeremiah mentions backsliding 13 times (2:19, 3:6-22, 5:6, 8:5, 14:7, 31:22, 49:4). The word "prophet" is mentioned over 71 times in the New Testament. Prophet is the other half of the foundation of the church. (Eph. 2:20).

The Prophet Prepares the Way for the Apostle

Matthew 3:3, "The voice of one crying in the wilderness, prepare ye the way of the Lord, make his paths straight." Hebrews 3:1, "Wherefore, holy brethren, partakers of the heavenly calling, consider the Apostle and High Priest of our profession, Christ Jesus.?

The Prophet is Called to the Nations and Kingdoms.

The Prophet is second in rank and file in the New Testament Church (I Corinthians 12:28). Jeremiah 1:4-5, "Before I formed thee in the belly I knew thee; and before thou camest forth out of the womb I sanctified thee, and I ordained thee a prophet unto the nations."

Called and ordained before birth, in the mind of God,

Jeremiah 1:5, I Kings 19:18.

Set over nations and kingdoms . . . to bring judgment.

Jeremiah 1:10, Amos 7:8, I Peter 4:17.

What seest thou? (A seer) Jeremiah 1:11,

The Battle-ax of the Lord (A yoke breaker anointing) Jeremiah 51:20-64.

The prophet foretells.

"The word of the Lord which came unto Jeremiah from the Lord, when Nebuchadnezzar, King of Babylon and all his army, and all the kingdoms of the earth of his dominion, and all the people fought against Jerusalem and against all the cities thereof, saying, Thus saith the Lord, the God of Israel; Go and speak to Zedekiah king of Judah, and tell them, Thus saith the Lord; Behold, I will give this city into the hand of the king of Babylon, and he shall burn it with fire." Jeremiah 34:1-2.

PROPHETS

As we begin to examine several notable prophets of the Lord, we can clearly see how diverse they are. When we begin to define the Prophet ministry, we cannot stereotype it, or put it into our mold, model, or box. This will not work as we look into the complexity of the Prophet Ministry. From Elijah to Samuel the contrast is so different. Here Elijah, the Tishbite, was one of the greatest prophets of all time. He was raised up by God to come against one of the worst kings in Israel's history. Ahab and his wife Jezebel were zealous Baal worshippers. This led to the official endorsement of this immoral and idolatrous form of worship. In effect, Baal was believed to control the rain. This is why God would raise up a prophet like Elijah, who would challenge Baal by commanding the rain to cease for over three years. Then after three years this prophet Elijah would come to Israel and challenge not only Baal, but also Ahab and 450 false prophets upon Mount Carmel. Thus Elijah would prove that Baal was a false God. Then he would execute 450 false prophets, then run in fear from Jezebel, hide in a cave and wish to die (what a contrast).

Now Samuel, in contrast, is a different story. He was a promised vow of his mother Hannah, who hand delivered him to the Priest Eli. He would minister in the Temple of the Lord for many years and still not know the Lord's voice. This young Samuel would inherit the ministry of Eli, because Eli refused to discipline his sons, thus stopping the line of succession. Samuel also was one of the greatest prophets of all times. God called Samuel four times before he answered the call. Each time that God called, Samuel would go back to his mentor and ask, Did you call me? We must clearly understand and realize that no man can call a prophet; only God can call a prophet. Man can only confirm. No school can birth a prophet; they can only train those that have been called by God.

This is one of the most awesome commentaries in all bible history . . . listen to these words. I Samuel 3:19-20, "And Samuel grew, and the Lord was with him, and did let none of his words fall to the ground. And all Israel from Dan even to Beersheba knew that Samuel was established to be a prophet of the Lord."

Samuel anointed Saul to be the first king of all Israel, and then picked David to be his successor. What a legacy these two prophets left. Elijah and Samuel were both chosen by God, but had totally different ministries. Let this be a firm lesson to the believer when examining the 21st Century ministry of the prophet.

Let's examine several notable prophets

Elijah—caused it not to rain for over three years (I Kings 17:1).

- Commanded the widow woman to fetch and to feed him first. Her meal barrel did not wax empty. (I Kings 17:15).
- Hides in a cave; and wishes to die. (I Kings 19:9)
- Rides up into heaven, in a fiery chariot. (II Kings 2:11)

Jeremiah—called by God, sanctified by God, ordained by God, set in position by God. (Jeremiah 1:5-10).

Samuel—Promised to the Lord. (I Samuel 1:11).

Ministered to the Lord. (I Samuel 3:11).

Called by God four times. (I Samuel 3:4-10).

God honored his word all his life. (I Samuel 3:19).

Anointed Kings. (I Samuel 10:1, 16:13).

Deborah—Judge over Israel, prophetess, and warrior. (Judges 4-5).

Gave Barak a command from the Lord. (Judges 4:6).

I will not go if thou go not with me. (Judges 4:8).

Isaiah—The bold pronouncement of death . . . from a senior prophet to the King of Judah . . . must be believed and received . . . because the senior prophet has a history of credibility, and that he speaks for the Lord.

Amos—And the Lord took me as I followed the flock, and the Lord said unto me, Go prophesy unto my people Israel. (Amos 7:15).

God speaks to His prophets first. (Amos 3:7).

Who can but prophesy? (Amos 3:8).

Do not prophesy at Bethel. (Amos 7:13)

Isaiah pronounces a death sentence to Hezekiah . . . (Only a true prophet could have such boldness). In II Kings 20:1-3, we read that "In those days was Hezekiah sick unto death. And the prophet Isaiah the son of Amoz came to him, and said unto him, Thus saith the Lord, Set thine house in order; for thou shalt die, and not live. Then he turned his face to the wall, and prayed unto the Lord, saying, I beseech thee, O Lord, remember now how I have walked before thee in truth and with a perfect heart, and have done that which is good in thy sight. And Hezekiah wept sore." II Kings 20:6, "And I will add unto thy days fifteen years; and I will deliver thee and this city out of the hands of the king of Assyria, and I will defend this city for mine own sake, and for my servant David's sake."

The Office of the Prophet

Ezekiel 1:1, "Now it came to pass in the thirtieth year, in the fourth month, in the fifth day of the month, as I was among the captives by the river of Chebar, that the heavens were opened, and I saw visions of God." Verse 3, "The word of the Lord came expressly unto Ezekiel the priest, the son of Buzi, in the land of the Chaldeans by the river Chebar; and the hand of the Lord was there upon him.

1. Saw visions

2. The word of the Lord came expressly unto Ezekiel

3. The hand of the Lord was there upon him.

Ezekiel 37:1, "The hand of the Lord was upon me, and carried me out in the spirit of the Lord and set me down in the midst of the valley which was full of bones."

Five ways to Identify a Prophet

1. Men of God—I Samuel 9:6, I Kings 12:22. They follow, declare, and uphold the ways of God

2. Seers—I Samuel 9:6, II Chronicles 33:18, II Samuel 24:11, Amos 7:12, Isaiah 29:10. The prophet is a seer because of the visions, insight, and foresight, which they receive from the Lord for the people.

3. Interpreters—Isaiah 43:27. They interpreted the history of the nation in the light of the word of the Lord. Interpreters of the law of the Lord. Interpreters of dreams. (Daniel 2:28), "But there is a God in heaven that revealeth secrets, and maketh known to the King Nebuchadnezzar . . ."

4. Messengers of the Lord—Isaiah 43:19, Malachi 3:1. Every prophet should have a divine message from God, bearing

the messages of the Lord to the nation, speaking under the inspiration of the Holy Spirit.

5. Servants—Haggai 2:3. Love—slaves to the will and service of God. All prophets must have an active prayer life and given to worship. Prayer and worship are the demonstration of the love relationship that the prophet has with Jehovah.

Is There a Prophet among You?

As we come together and begin to discern the giftings of the house, it is imperative that we begin to dialogue with the Set-Man, Founder, or Visionary of each house to assess and confirm the charisma of each individual, their maturity, and level of gifting. The sphere is so vast it would be an injustice to stereotype or put our analysis in a category from 1 to 10. In our best efforts we would like you, the reader, to understand it. It is like trying to compare the different states in America. For instance, Arizona with Pennsylvania, or New York with Hawaii, or Texas with Alaska; at best we can assimilate they are all states of the union, but very different in scope, application, or function. We come together with the set man of this house and confirm the junior prophetess and the prophet in training . . . the wild undisciplined prophet . . . or the Prophet of God who is ready to be loosed.

Is there a Prophet among you? There are a few things we can do in our best efforts. One is to separate those that have the gift of prophecy with those that are called to be prophets. Number one, a prophet should be operating or show signs of operating in at least four gifts of the Spirit, especially the revelation gifts, and a power gift or two. The 21st Century prophet should have a seasoned mentor or father that he or she serves. There is no better training than to serve a seasoned man or woman of God. Is there a prophet among you? Are you willing to set your vision aside and serve as a pure servant in the capacity of a minister to an Elijah or a Moses? Can you serve as an Armor Bearer; follow a king like Saul to fulfill your destiny? Can you be an inner circle disciple, like Peter, James, and John, then fall short and go back to business as usual—**then** hear the voice of God and run to your upper room destiny? A Prophet will have many pitfalls and shortcomings, but one thing will be certain, he will know the voice of God (Amos 3:7).

II Kings 3:11, "But Jehoshaphat said, Is there not here a prophet of the Lord, that we may enquire of the Lord by him? And one of the king of Israel's servants answered and said, Here is Elisha the son of Shaphat, which poured water on the hands of Elijah." This is servant hood personified, where Elisha, who left his natural father and mother to serve his spiritual father, Elijah, is now being summoned by King Jehoshaphat. At last all these years of servitude have become his badge of honor.

Isaiah 6:8, "Also I heard the voice of the Lord, saying, whom shall I send, and who will go for us? Then said I, Here am I; send me."

John 15:16, "Ye have not chosen me, but I have chosen you, and ordained you, that ye should go and bring forth fruit: and that your fruit should remain." The word chose here means commissioned. The word commission means to be launched out, sent forth by government or governing power, such as the kingdom of God and one of his established agents, such as an apostle or prophet.

Matthew 20:16, "So the last shall be first, and the first shall be last: for many are called, but few chosen."

Amos 7:14-15, "Then answered Amos, and said to Amaziah, I was no prophet, neither was I a prophet's son; but I was an herdsman, and a gatherer of sycamore fruit: And the Lord took me as I followed the flock, and the Lord said unto me, Go, prophesy unto my people Israel." An exception to the rule of being commissioned; every once in a while God will select an Amos who does not have a legacy or heritage, just a divine call from God. Be careful not to let tradition or religion box you in, thus stereotyping your understanding of the prophet's ministry, for there are so many variations.

How Can We Recognize False Prophets?

Matthew 7:16-20, Jesus said that, "Ye shall know them by their fruits. Do men gather grapes of thorns, or figs of thistles? Even so every good tree bringeth forth good fruit; but a corrupt tree bringeth forth evil fruit. A good tree cannot bring forth evil fruit . . . wherefore by their fruits ye shall know them."

I John 4:1, "Beloved, believe not every spirit, but try the spirits whether they are of God: because many false prophets are gone out into the world."

The Gift of Prophecy

Greek: "propheteia" a noun that signifies the speaking forth of the mind and counsel of God. It is the declaration of that which cannot be known by natural means. It is the forth-telling of the will of God, whether with reference to the past, the present, or the future." (Vines, p. 893)

In Joel 2:28 the word of God says, "And it shall come to pass afterward, that I will pour out my spirit upon all flesh; and your sons and your daughters shall prophesy, your old men shall dream dreams, your young men shall see visions." The gift of prophecy was prophesied by Joel to sons and daughters as a future realization. On the day of Pentecost it finally came to a reality. The saints were in the upper room and suddenly a sound came from Heaven as of a rushing mighty wind. During this occurrence they were all filled with the Holy Ghost and began to speak with other tongues. The Apostle Peter stood up on that day and began to explain this phenomenon. (Acts 2:16-18), "But this is that which was spoken by the Prophet Joel; and it shall come to pass in the last days, saith God, I will pour out of my Spirit upon all flesh: and your sons and your daughters shall prophesy . . ."

The whole church has the ability to prophesy. In John 1:12 it says, "But as many as received Him, to them He gave power to become sons of God . . ." The outpouring has been available to the church since the day of Pentecost, and will be available henceforth.

The Apostle Paul better explains the gift of prophecy in I Corinthians 14:1. He states, "Follow after charity, and desire spiritual gifts, but rather that ye may prophesy." He is clearly saying to the church that the gift of prophecy far outweighs the other eight gifts of the Spirit. As we begin to understand the power of the spoken word, Proverbs 18:21 comes to mind . . . "Death and life are in the power of the tongue." We as saints have the ability to produce life. The prophetic gift of prophecy in no way makes one a Prophet. The gift of prophesy, according to I Corinthians 14:3, has certain boundaries, which are edification, exhortation, and comfort. The gift of prophecy should never bring judgment. This sometimes harsh reality belongs to the seasoned prophet.

New Testament prophecy functions in three realms. The scriptures stress that the gift of prophecy is the most important gift. Paul said, under the inspiration of the Holy Spirit, greater is he that prophesieth than he that speaketh with tongues, (I Corinthians 14:5), so prophecy would have to be greater than tongues, except he interpret. The gift of prophecy often is confused with the Office of the Prophet. There is a ministry of the Prophet, but not everyone who prophesies is a prophet. A rich man has money. Although I may have some money in my wallet, that does not make me a rich man. You may prophesy, but operating the simple gift of prophecy does not qualify you to stand in the office of a prophet. Naturally, a prophet would have this gift of prophecy in operation, but he also has some of the gifts of revelation. To stand in the office of a Prophet, one must have a consistent manifestation of at least two of the revelation gifts (word of wisdom, word of knowledge, or discerning of spirits) plus prophecy. We can see that the prophetic gift is different from the office of a Prophet because Paul encouraged the whole church at Corinth to covet to prophecy (I Corinthians 14:1). He already had stated in the 12th Chapter of I Corinthians that God had set these different ministries in the church, so he's not telling everyone to seek the office of a Prophet. Instead, he's telling them that all may prophecy.

In the 21st Chapter of Acts, Luke records that Paul and his company went down to Caesarea and entered the house of Philip, the evangelist. The scriptures tell us that Philip had four daughters who prophesied. It does not call them prophetesses. In the same chapter a senior prophet, Agabus, took Paul's girdle and told him what he was about to suffer. Well, the word suffer does not fall in the category of the gift of prophesy. Suffering does not compare to the standard the Apostle Paul gives to the gift of prophesy; that is, edification, exhortation, and comfort. Suffering, rebuke, and correction are reserved for the prophet, not those who prophesy.

Prophecy vs. Preaching

There are many theologians and denominations who still teach that preaching and prophesying are the same. We must sharply disagree. To "preach" means to proclaim, to announce, to cry, and to tell. Jesus said, go ye into all the world, and preach the gospel (Mark 16:15). He didn't say to prophesy the gospel. Likewise, Paul did not say that men will be saved by the foolishness of prophesying. He said they will be saved, "by the foolishness of preaching" (I Corinthians 1:21)

Preach, Preaching

There are three words in the Greek that we would like you, the reader, to examine in your Vines dictionary. The first word is taken from Matthew 3:1 and Matthew 4:17. Preach, Preaching

= Greek, Kerusso (2784) signifies to be a herald or in general to proclaim, not prophecy. Greek, Prokerusso (4296) To proclaim as a herald. Acts 13:24 Greek, Kerugma (2782) a proclamation by a herald denotes a message. Mark 16:15 says, "Go ye into all the world, and preach the gospel to every creature." I Corinthians 1:21, "For after that in the wisdom of God the world by wisdom knew not God, it pleased God by the foolishness of preaching to save them that believed"—not prophesy.

The Testimony of Christ

Jesus gives inspired testimony and praise through His saints by prophetic utterance or songs of the Lord. Revelation 19:10, "for the testimony of Jesus is the spirit of prophecy." Ephesians 5:19, ". . . speaking to yourselves in psalms and hymns and spiritual songs." One of the manifestations of the Holy Spirit is called the gift of prophecy. There are nine gifts of the Spirit, which bring edification, exhortation, and comfort to the body of Christ with gifts that differ (I Corinthians 12:10). Romans 12:6, "Having then gifts differing according to the grace that is given to us, whether prophecy, let us prophesy according to the proportion of faith." The Prophet speaking by divine utterance speaks the mind and counsels of God and gives a rhema word for edification, direction, correction, confirmation, and instruction in righteousness (I Corinthians 14:29; II Timothy 3:16-17). A truly divinely inspired prophecy is the Holy Spirit expressing the thoughts and desires of Christ through a human voice.

I Corinthians 12:1, "Now concerning spiritual gifts, brethren, I would not have you ignorant."

I Corinthians 14:1, "Follow after charity, and desire spiritual gifts, but rather that ye may prophesy"

I Corinthians 14:3, "But he that prophesieth speaketh unto men to edification, exhortation, and comfort."

Job Description: Joel 2:28, "And it shall come to pass that afterwards I will pour out my spirit upon all flesh; and your sons and daughters shall prophesy."

Romans 12:6, "Having then gifts differing according to the grace that is given to us, whether prophesy, let us prophesy according to the proportion of faith."

Gifts of the Spirit (I Corinthians 12:7-11).

Gifts of Revelation

Word of Knowledge

Word of Wisdom

Gift of discernment

Power Gifts

Gift of Faith

Working of Miracles

Gifts of Healings

Gifts of Utterance

Diverse Kinds of Tongues

Interpretation of Tongues

Prophecy

Chapter 5

MINISTRY OF HELPS PASTORS AND EVANGELISTS

In Ephesians 4:11 the word of God says, "And he gave some, apostles; and some, prophets; and some, evangelists; and some, pastors and teachers." Let us take a look at the office of the evangelist for a moment using I Corinthians 12:28 as our reference, "And God hath set some in the church, first apostles, secondarily prophets, thirdly teachers, after that miracles, then gifts of healings, **helps,** governments, diversities of tongues.

As we begin to examine this scripture we can clearly see the **evangelist** is not visible as an entity. It is here, but now falls into a category when God is setting divine order. This category is **helps**. Along with the pastor, the evangelist is a help to the church universal in order to give more enlightenment. Let's look at the next word after helps, which is governments.

Governments, Greek word, Kubernesis (2941) from Kubernao, to guide, steer, pilot. Metaphorically, governments or governing, as those who act as a guide in a local church, Bishops, Elders and deacons. The evangelist acts as one who brings converts into the local church and recovers those who have become weary in well doing.

As I, the Apostle M.P. Sterling, embark on this very controversial trail, I hope that you, the reader, would bear with me once again with an open mind. For if the church is to be one, as prescribed by our predecessors, it is our hope that you would receive illumination, revelation, and understanding to know that when I speak, I can only speak to the church universal, the one, united church with different administrations, different operations, but the same Lord and the same Spirit.

I sit here today in Liberia, West Africa, June 20, 2006, 4:00 am Liberian time about to begin my third rewrite on this chapter. I understand it clearly, but it is this humble writer's endeavor to communicate what God has shown me—that the church is really one church. (smile).

If we look at the church from a denominational point there is a split in the hierarchy. And the word of God says that a house divided against itself cannot stand. Do you want the church to be continually anemic? A place where the blood and anointing is weak and without power? Do you really care more about God's church than your own church and denomination?

Often times, as I read this particular scripture, I wondered why Pastors and Evangelists were not mentioned. Then one day God spoke to me and said they are there, right in front of your eyes, but because your conception of the church is singular in scope, you cannot see. Understand the church universal, with few apostles and prophets, with many pastors who tend my sheepfolds; many pens, one church . . . ministry of helps to my church, which is broad in scope.

Vine's dictionary words for "helps" are "antilepsis or antilempis." It is mentioned in I Corinthians 12:28 as one of the ministrations in the local church, by way of rendering assistance, perhaps especially of help ministering to the weak and needy, Pastor/Shepherd.

Pastors

Pastors guide as well as feed the flock. This involves tender care and is a help to the body of Christ, when you start to understand the big picture. These Utopian Shepherds have lorded over God's people with almost no accountability, and through their self-seeking grandiose posture have caused many schisms throughout the body of Christ; thus, an erosion of the unity of the Spirit occurs. In the body of Christ or the Church Universal you must understand when we talk about the church, we are taking about the church as a whole, not a division of denominational separatism. In I Corinthians 12 the Apostle Paul starts off by saying, "Now concerning spiritual gifts brethren, I would not have you ignorant." Verses 4-6, "Now, there are diversities of gifts, but the same Spirit. And there are differences of administrations, but the same Lord. And there are diversities of operations, but it is the same God which worketh all in all." Verse 12, "For as the body is one, and hath many members, and all the members of that one body, being many, are one body: so also is Christ." Verse 20, "But now are they many members, yet but one body." You many know all this. My answer in question form is: How can I tell? The bible says that faith without works is dead, so, if you know these things and are not moving toward Christ as your center and allow yourself to remain separated from His Body, then you are anti-Christ or anti His body coming together. Saints of God, we must get back to the Bible and start to do it the Bible way.

The Evangelist

A messenger of the Gospel denotes a preacher, a revivalist, one who converts a non-believer to Christianity. The word "evangelist" is found three times in the bible.

The Middle Finger represents the Evangelist, not by rank and file, but in position for this illustration. The Evangelist is far reaching, that middle finger that is the longest on the fivefold ministry hand of God. The Evangelist in divine order has the power to snatch souls from the kingdom of darkness and translate them into the kingdom of light. This Evangelist is a soul saver, an exhorter to the body of Christ. The time of the Lone Ranger, and non-accountability, is drawing to an end. This gift must come into divine order, submitting to an Apostolic father for rest, covering, and revelation concerning the current move or moves of God worldwide, or even in the region he is currently in, or is about to be sent. There is an apostolic wind moving across the land at an alarming rate. It reminds me of a snowball on top of a mountain, starting off small, moving slowly down the hill, picking up momentum as it grows ever larger, while affecting everything old in its path, covering all with a blanket of pure white snow. I heard it said in times of old, a single spark could start a prairie fire.

In II Timothy 4:5, the Apostle Paul exhorts Timothy to do the work of an Evangelist, making full proof of his ministry. The Evangelist is one who begins to make converts. The Apostle Paul is saying to Timothy to spread the good news, win souls to Christ. This will make full proof of your ministry. The word of God says in Proverbs 11:30, "The fruit of the righteous is a tree of life; and he that winneth souls is wise." This conversion process is for all the saints, but is a particular calling for the Evangelist. Even in Joshua's time, he saved Rahab the harlot, and it is believed she was converted. So it is essential that we continue to advance the invisible kingdom by bringing souls under its authority, whereby Jesus is made Lord of their life.

Romans 10:14-15, "How then shall they call on him in whom they have not believed? And how shall they believe in Him of whom they have not heard? And how shall they hear without a preacher? And how shall they preach, except they be sent? As it is written, How beautiful are the feet of them that preach the gospel of peace, and bring glad tidings of good things!"

The Evangelist is one of the fivefold ministry's preaching gifts. Some are called to travel all over the country, while others are called worldwide, while some are even assigned to the local church and community. In I Corinthians 12:28 we find helps and government. We believe that the Evangelist is a part of the ministry of helps to the church universal. Also in Acts 21:8, Philip, one of the original deacons, is now called an evangelist. He has advanced in ministry. Paul and his company stayed at his house for several days. He also had four daughters, which prophesied. The Joel 2:28 anointing has come upon his house. His ministry is flourishing. This evangelist is also seen in the book of Acts in the eighth chapter converting the Ethiopian Eunuch to Christianity, preaching Jesus unto him and baptizing him also.

We must begin to understand that the Evangelist is the one who preaches and converts souls into the Kingdom of God. Timothy is told to prove his ministry. How? By saving souls. So if you are called to preach, before you ask for the pulpit ministry, prove your ministry by leading souls to Christ. Convert your family, neighbors, and your community to Christ. This will establish your ministry while advancing the Kingdom of God.

Pastor

The word "pastor" is not mentioned in the New Testament bible in singular form; however, the word "pastors" in plural form is mentioned only once. Shepherd is mentioned 14 times. The Ring Finger represents the Pastor (Shepherd). He is married to the flock or sheep. It is his job to keep the flock together. I think if you begin to see the church in a broader sense instead of one building or edifice being looked at as the church; it's merely one sheep pen or one fold. John 10:16, "And other sheep I have, which are not of this fold: Them also I must bring, and they shall hear my voice; and there shall be one fold, and one shepherd."

The church consists of multiple entities in collaboration of spirit. The different church buildings or sheep pens have different shepherds/pastors. These shepherds were never meant to run the church, merely to tend the sheep of his flock.

Let us examine type and shadow—David the shepherd in I Samuel 16:11, "And Samuel said unto Jesse, are here all thy children? And he said, There remaineth yet the youngest, and, behold, he keepeth the sheep. And Samuel said unto Jesse, Send and fetch him: for we will not sit down till he come hither." In this scene we can see again the shadow of the church or the nation appearing.

If we dare to look hard beyond our religiosity, there emerges the shadow of the fivefold, that is, Samuel as the prophet of God. Jesse symbolizes apostolic authority, a fathering spirit over his vast holdings. And David, the eighth son, as a keeper of his flock, he was a pastor over his father's sheep. Webster's Dictionary defines the word Keeper or Keepeth as one who guards or watches, a person who assumes responsibility for another. Tend is to watch over and care for, minister to, to attend to by work or service.

I Samuel 17:15, "But David went and returned from Saul to feed his father's sheep at Bethlehem." Jessie was not the shepherd, David was. David guarded over the sheep: He assumed responsibility for the sheep when the wolf, lion, or bear came, but they were his father's sheep. In Hebrew the word ra'ah is to tend a flock. Greek poimaino, shepherd. (Webster's) shepherd—a person who herds, tends, and guards sheep. I Samuel 17:34-35, "And David said unto Saul, Thy servant kept his father's sheep, and there came a lion, and a bear, and took a lamb out of the flock: And I went out after him, and smote him, and delivered it out of his mouth: And when he arose against me, I caught him by his beard, and smote him, and slew him."

In the book of Luke 16:12 the word of God says, "And as ye have not been faithful in that which is another man's, who shall give you that which is your own?" David, the good shepherd, says to King Saul, this is my resume. I have been faithful over my father's sheep to the point that I risked my life for his flock. When the lion came, I proved myself faithful over my father's pasture, and I will be faithful over this Kingdom business.

We must begin to understand that Kingdom business is more important than shepherding over one local assembly. We have been so concerned about our local assembly, that the Kingdom of God is suffering, or divided. There is only one church, and we're all members of the multi-membered, culturally diverse, corporate body of Christ. Each shepherd of today's church needs an apostolic father to cover his ministry; also to speak into his life and prepare him for the high calling. David had been anointed by the Prophet Samuel while still tending his father's sheep. He was now anointed for his purpose, on his way to destiny.

His destiny was not to tend sheep, but to be King over a nation. Moses, having studied at the best school in Egypt, was ill prepared for the task at hand. He was to lead a nation out of bondage into the promises of God. First, he had to run out of Egypt to the backside of the mountain and to remain there for 40 years. There he learned shepherding. He was faithful over Jethro's sheep, another typology of an apostle, who would advise him through purpose, and walk with him toward destiny. Jethro, his father-in-law, would advise him before his departure to his own land. He advised that the multitude is too heavy or too much to bear alone. So Moses hearkened unto the counsel of this Apostolic Father and began to appoint faithful men over thousands, hundreds, and rulers over fifty, and they judged the people. Thus Moses has received the apostolic mandate and placed the shepherds over the nation.

Bishop Earl Paulk, Cathedral of the Holy Spirit at Chapel Hill, Decatur, Georgia, had a multi-member conglomeration of shepherds on staff, some over thousands and others over several hundreds. The types and shadows that we have examined will further give us illustrations that will bring us into the understanding of the ultimate kingdom. There is a clear picture emerging, if we would begin to look beyond our religious tradition and denominational policies. King Saul and the nation of Israel represent a typology of the external kingdom, which is presently manifesting in the earth realm. Daniel 4:3 and Revelation 11:15 begin to unfold the mystery of the kingdom of God. Even in the Lord's Prayer we prophetically begin to proclaim it, Thy kingdom come in earth. But this is another subject for another time.

Jessie, David's father represents the apostolic covering that has vast holdings, an apostolic supply. He has a bakery, a dairy, vineyards, a winery, pastures, carriages, servants, and much more. Jessie is not only raising sons to help advance the kingdom, he is also sending corn, cheese, bread, and wine to the captains along with their pledge. (I Samuel 17:17, 18.) His three eldest sons enjoy the primo job of serving in Saul's army, while David had the menial job of just watching over the sheep. Why do you think when the prophet of God, Samuel, came to Jessie's realm David was not called out with the seven other children? It was not until God assured the prophet that the next King was not among the seven that he inquired, Is there another? David was an afterthought. We have put so much emphasis on the pastor/shepherd and the local assembly that we've lost the big picture.

The big picture is this: If you are a pastor or shepherd, have you slain your lion and killed your bear? Are you now ready to face your giant? Everything else was preparation. Destiny is calling you. Your Goliath, the kingdom of darkness, and the kingdoms of this world are challenging the anointing in your life. Will you play it safe behind those four walls, or march into Egypt and tell Pharaoh, "Let my people go"?

The Kingdom of God suffers violence and the violent taketh it by force. The Kingdom of God is suffering because so many men, powerful men and women of God, have been caught in the pastoral trap. Some of the Fivefold ministry gifts have become ineffective, having been placed in a pastoral position—due to the lack of cohesion in the church universal, where the multi-membered, culturally diverse, corporate body of Christ profits withal.

I Corinthians 12:6-7, "And there are diversities of operations, but it is the same God which worketh all in all . . . But the manifestation of the Spirit is given to every man to profit withal." We're all supposed to profit from each one's gift and calling. And the laborer is worth his reward. It's time out for the grand-standing pastor issuing out peanuts at his discretion to the apostle, prophet, master teacher and evangelist. This was not God's fivefold ministry plan along with these denominational Bishops. There is no care for the fivefold ministry gifts that our Lord and Savior Jesus Christ gave, to perfect the saints for the work of the ministry. In most cases these utopian Pastors are the only ones benefiting from the Priesthood blessing. If we would look at the Levitical priesthood, which is our schoolmaster, we would clearly understand there must be a form of equity in the church. A pastor's heart is not capable of this endeavor; only an Apostolic Father would have a father's heart for the multi-membered, culturally diverse, corporate body of Christ (The church). We as God's governmental leaders must begin to reshape the role of tomorrow's pastors . . . today. I will begin by calling them shepherds. I reiterate the word "pastor" in the singular is not found at all in the New Testament Bible, while the apostle and prophet in some form or another are found over 150 times. Some of you need to begin to wonder why? If the Bible is our compass and guide, why would it place so little emphasis on the word "pastor" by leaving the word completely out of the New Testament, only to be found in plural form in Ephesians 4:11 along with the other Fivefold ministry offices, which are mentioned in some form or another in a combined total of over 200 times. There is something wrong with this picture, and it does not take a rocket scientist to figure it out. I hope this provokes you to thought and moves you to action, saints of God. This is a revolution, a time for change.

Martin Luther King, Jr.—A Jeremiah Prophet

Dr. King was a true prophet of God, but was known locally as co-pastor of Ebenezer Baptist Church, where his father was senior pastor. What if he had pursued the pastorate, instead of being placed over nations and kingdoms to root out the demon of racism, or to pull down the principalities of hatred, or destroy the lies of segregation, and throw down the idolatrous nature of violence? Yes, this prophet of God would begin to build race relationships and plant seeds of brotherhood. Jeremiah 1:10, "See I have set you this day over nations and kingdoms, to root out and pull down and to destroy and to throw down, to build and to plant. Moreover the word of the Lord came unto me saying Jeremiah, what seest thou? And I said, I see the rod of an almond tree." Now we all know what Dr. Martin Luther King, Jr., the prophet of God, saw. He said he went to the mountaintop and saw the promise land!

Yes! I reiterate. What if Dr. King had pursued the pastorate instead of being called to the nations as a prophet of God? Yes,

yes, yes! He was a prophet, even if he did not realize it. I, Michael Paul Sterling, clearly see all the earmarks and ultimate death of this great 21st Century prophet.

Many apostles, prophets, and master teachers have pursued the pastorate at their own peril. Many times years later, having unfulfilled ministries, they are found spiritually dead in the wilderness of despair, having tried on armor that does not fit.

What about the loss to us as a people when one has success—out of his calling? We all lose, because everyone knows that good is the enemy of best. Examine yourself; the kingdom of God and all creation awaits the manifestation of the sons of God. Are you one of those who now realize that the pastorate is not your flow? You have been functioning, but it's not where you are excelling. It simply means that you have been caught in the pastoral trap. There is a solution. The Apostle and Prophet have come home. They have a fathering spirit and divine direction. It's time for re-classification. Contact us: we will help salvage the ministry and propel you to your divine calling.

Recently while helping a Pastor/Master-Teacher save his church during a 30-day revival, he came to me after observing one of our Fivefold ministry teams in action and asked me to take over his church. I informed him that I had not come for that purpose. He asked me to carefully consider the matter. He explained that he had gotten caught in the pastoral trap. He is now teaching seminars, and is excited about the future. We have placed a shepherd in the house and have ordained eldership. The church is now growing rapidly.

Chapter 6

FIVEFOLD MINISTRY TEACHERS

I Corinthians 12:28, "And God set some in the church, first apostles, secondarily prophets, and thirdly teachers." The Office of Teacher is third in rank and file, having been set in the church by God. The word teacher is mentioned four times in the New Testament in singular form, and 20 times in one form or another, while pastor is mentioned only one time.

The Little Finger represents the Teacher when examining the hand of God. The little finger is small, but so important in the Fivefold ministry. It is the teacher who leads and guides in all truth. The teacher or the Master Teacher is the one who receives revelation from apostolic and prophetic authority and breaks it down for all to understand. In the Word of Faith movement, there have been phenomenal teachers who have come on the scene, literally teaching God's word with not a lot of exhortation or preaching, but teaching line upon line, precept upon precept.

When the teacher begins to teach stale manna, it is because there is neither rhema nor revelation.

Master Teacher—The Teacher of Revelation

It is my contention that revelation into God's Word only comes through apostolic and prophetic order. Reference Ephesians 3:5, "Which in other ages was not made known unto the sons of men as it is now revealed unto His holy apostles and prophets by the spirit." The word "teacher" in the Greek is did-as-kal-os. The meaning of this word gives us a closer insight into this powerful office. First of all we need to understand that the word "teacher" is translated 48 times "master" in the New Testament; therefore we have coined the word "Master Teacher". It is also translated as doctor, or instructor. In the book of Acts 5:34 it says, "Then stood there up one in the council, a Pharisee, named Gamaliel, a doctor of the law . . ." The Greek word for doctor, nom-od-id-kal-os, is translated here as an expounder of the Jewish Law, a rabbi-doctor (teacher) of the law. When the Apostle Paul states in Hebrews 5:12, By this time ye ought to be teachers (masters, doctors, instructors), we get a better insight, to understand that they had not mastered the word, having sat in the pews

15-20 years. Like so many churchgoers today, they come to church on Sunday, but are not walking epistles. Some of the believers do not carry their bibles, let alone read the context therein. II Timothy 2:15 says, "Study to shew thyself approved unto God, a workman that needeth not to be ashamed, rightly dividing the word of truth." Do you still believe that the bible says cleanliness is next to Godliness? The Master Teacher is so important to the next move of God. It is necessary that the Master Teacher takes his/her rightful place in the Fivefold Ministry. I have seen many, many men and women of God called as Master Teachers trying to pastor, or be an apostle, when their true calling is as a Master Teacher, doctor, or instructor. Do not misunderstand me, I believe that those called to the fivefold ministry can have dual functions, but one is always primary. If we would flow in the primary function, then everything else would work in a harmonic fashion and balance that would indeed edify the church and all of its parts. Everything needs to flow in divine order. When we begin to see the fivefold ministry of the apostle, prophet, evangelist, pastor and teacher coming into its full maturity, restoration, and divine order, then the very plan of God according to the blueprint can manifest, and we can stop the confusion. This has plagued the church and caused the division, which is now at work.

The confusion started when those, who were not called, started writing all those books and commentaries about what the bible is saying. Some of the teachings are so far off base that when the simple truth comes, it seems as if it is from outer space somewhere. But alas, have no fear, for the Bible says, my sheep hear my voice and no other voice will they follow. When the Master Teachers start to teach the revelation to the evangelist and pastor that have flowed down from the apostle and prophet, they will be in line for true revival. We will all be saying the same thing to the sheep, and the body will start to be edified.

The Master Teacher must sit at the feet of the Apostles and Prophets and assimilate revelation. You can see the image and the shadow of the precept in Nehemiah 8:2-4, "And Ezra the priest brought the law before the congregation both of men and women, and all that could hear with understanding, upon the first day of the seventh month. And he read therein before the street that was before the water gate from the morning until midday, before men and women and those that could understand; and the ears of all the people were attentive unto the book of the law. And Ezra the scribe stood upon a pulpit of wood, which they had made for that purpose . . ." In this scene Ezra, the Scribe, stands at the pulpit and teaches the law to a few chosen men, who in turn teach the populace. Verses 7-8, "Also Jeshua, and Bani and Sherebiah, Jamin, Akkub, Shabbethai, Hodijah, Maaseiah, Kelita, Azariah, Jozabad, Hanan, Pelaiah, and the Levites, caused the people to understand the law: and the people stood in their place. So they read in the book in the law of God distinctly, and gave the sense, and caused them to understand the reading."

In the book of John in the 3rd chapter, it says that a certain ruler of the Jews came to Jesus by night, and the first word from Nicodemus was Rabbi (Teacher). "We know that thou art a teacher come from God, for no one can do these miracles that thou doest except God be with him." The Master Teacher under God's designated authority will walk in full manifestation of son-ship. This divine order of God's plan must come into fruition, so that the multi-member corporate body of Christ will begin to do the greater works.

In the book of Romans 12:5-7, "So we, being many, are one body in Christ, and everyone members one of another. Having then gifts differing according to the grace that is given unto us, whether prophecy, let us prophesy according to the proportion of faith; Or ministry, let us wait on our ministering; or he that teacheth, on teaching." Hebrews 5:4 says, "And no man taketh this honor upon himself, but he that is called of God, as was

Aaron." It's "time out" for a bunch of renegade bastard teachers from some street prophecy without proper oversight. Woe to those who rebelliously refuse to be covered and have not been taught. Bastard means to be without a father or headship, just some illegitimate conception in the back alley or in the back seat of a revival or convention, where as an undisciplined teacher you went, but were not sent, called, or confirmed. Wait teacher on teaching.

It further states in Hebrews 5:12-14, "For when for the time ye ought to be teachers, ye have need that one teach you again which be the first principles of the oracles of God; and are become such as have need of milk, and not of strong meat. For everyone that useth milk is unskillful in the word or righteousness: for he is a babe. But strong meat belongeth to them that are of full age, even those who by reason of use have their senses exercised to discern both good and evil." The writer is saying you ought to be teachers, but you have need that someone teach you again. Go find an apostolic father (apostle), and sit at his feet and learn the six doctrinal principles of Christ, and then let him send you, Master Teacher, with understanding and revelation.

King David says in Psalms 119:99-100, "I have more understanding than all my teachers: for all thy testimonies are my meditation. I understand more than the ancients, because I keep thy precepts."

Teacher, an Instructor of Truth

"All scripture is given by inspiration of God, and is profitable for doctrine, for reproof, for correction, for instruction in righteousness: That the man of God may be perfect, thoroughly furnished unto all good works." (II Timothy 3:16-17). A New Testament Apostolic/Prophetic Teacher is one who not only teaches the letter of the word, but also ministers the rhema word under a holy anointing. He exhibits keen spiritual discernment and has divine insight into the word of God and its personal application to believers. II Corinthians 3:6, "Who also hath made us able ministers of the New Testament; not of the letter, but of the spirit, for the letter killeth, but the spirit giveth life."

II Timothy 2:2, "And the things that thou hast heard of me among many witnesses, the same commit thou to faithful men, who shall be able to teach others also."

II Timothy 2:15, "Study to shew thyself approved unto God, a workman that needeth not to be ashamed, rightly dividing the word of truth."

II Timothy 3:15, "And that from a child thou hast known the holy scriptures, which are able to make thee wise unto salvation through faith which is in Christ Jesus."

Logos & Rhema

Logos (Greek) "word"—the unchanging, inerrant, creative and inspired word of God. (See Psalm 119:89, "Forever, O Lord, thy word (logos) is settled in heaven.") Logos is the entire written Word of God—the Holy Bible. It is the complete revelation of God, His personage, character, plan and eternal purpose as we find in Scriptures.

Rhema, Greek "word"—derived from the verb "to speak". See Romans 10:17, "So then faith cometh by hearing, and hearing by the word (rhema) of God." Rhema is a word or an illustration God speaks directly to us, and it addresses our personal, particular situation. It is a timely, Holy Spirit inspired word for the logos that brings life, power and faith to perform and fulfill it. It's significance is exemplified in the injunction to take the "sword of the spirit, which is the word (rhema) of God." (Ephesians 6:17). It can be received through others such as by a prophetic word, or be an illumination given to one directly in their personal meditation and prayer. The logos is the fixed word of God, the scriptures, and the rhema is a particular portion in line with logos brought forth by the Spirit to be applied directly to something in our personal experience.

Chapter 7

RESTRUCTURING of THE CHURCH
THE ORDER OF BISHOPS

A Stolen Legacy

About 36 years after the death of Jesus Christ the first Apostle James, the brother of John, was slain. Thus begins the extinguishing of the Apostles of the Lamb. In about 80 A.D. Andrew the Apostle was crucified at Rome. During this time Nero, who fiddled while Rome burned down, was considered to be the Antichrist himself. James, the brother of the Lord, began to govern the church at Jerusalem along with the rest of the apostles. James had taken a Nazarite vow and so drank no wine nor did a razor touch his head. It is also said that he was a vegetarian and wore no woolen garments, and the only apostle that was allowed to enter the holy place, thus making him an apostle and priest after the manner of our Lord Jesus Christ. Hebrews 3:1, "Wherefore, holy brethren, partakers of the heavenly, consider the Apostle and High Priest of our profession, Christ Jesus." James, the brother of Jesus, was thrown down from the highest part of the temple, but did not die until struck in the head by a fellow, and ascended to his eternal reward. There is much to say of this period of martyrdom of the saints under Nero and his successor, Emperor Domitian, who exiled the Apostle John to the Isle of Patmos, where he was later released and died at a ripe old age. After the death of the Apostle Peter, a strange twist began as Ignatius was appointed to the Bishopric of Antioch. Thus, there was a broken legacy of apostles. No more will you hear the word apostle. Satan and his antichrists have stopped the true succession of apostles. No fault of the faithful Ignatius, Bishop of Antioch, who was also martyred in honorable fashion. But alas the foundation is halted as thousands of saints are martyred. We can see clearly an erosion of the apostle. The first ascension apostle, Paul, who was the first to be inaugurated after the death of Christ, had appointed Titus to be Bishop over the Isle of Crete, and Timothy over the Ephesus district. As Catholicism begins to flourish, the one whole government begins to come into view under Constantine. The apostolic and prophetic ministries vanish from view. The Word of God says unless a grain of wheat fall to the ground and dies, it abides alone. The germination period may have been long, but the apostles and prophets have been resurrected with a hundredfold return. A hundredfold return is that supernatural occurrence that does not come to those who claim it, but to those who are willing to pay the price.

As a 21st Century reformer and patriarch I can clearly see that the errors from Catholicism to the Reformation dealing with the issues of the hierarchy of the Bishop and its succession have never been addressed. The problem is found in the word succession itself. The word succession means this: the act of succeeding or coming after another in order or sequence to an office, estate, or throne. 2. The right to succeed to an office, estate, etc. (Webster's). As we examine the historical documents, we see the Apostle Peter ordaining (or appointing) by the laying on of hands Hermagoras as the Bishop of Aquileia, Italy. There as a witness was the Apostle Mark. We understand that he has the right to be the bishop under apostolic rule, not to succeed the Apostle. This usurping of power and authority is another step in destroying the apostle or apostolic authority in the church, as we further examine historical data through apostolic (enlightened) eyes. Let us take a closer examination of facts and data.

A **Bishop** (English derivation) from the New Testament Greek (episkopos) overseer, guardian, is an ordained or consecrated member of the clergy, who is generally entrusted with a position of authority and oversight within the church. For example, we look at Titus who was appointed by the apostle Paul over the churches of the isle of Crete, and Timothy who was appointed over the churches at Ephesus. We must understand that in these regions there were many cell groups but only one church.

As 21st century apostles begin to arise out of the darkness, it is incumbent that they have a divine encounter with Jesus Christ as Paul had on the road to Damascus. I'm not speaking of those that have been called, for many have been called but only a few shall be chosen. I'm speaking of those chosen as Ascension Apostles by the very voice of God, who can read and understand the blueprint of today's church through the revelation of scripture. For example, a type and shadow could be seen during the time of Moses, whose first encounter was the burning bush. God gives him a mission, a message, and the authority (exousia) to carry it out. Commissioned by God to go to Egypt and tell Pharaoh, let my people go, He also was given the full blueprint (as he ascended up Mount Sinai) of the tabernacle and all the furnishings, the outer court, the inner court, the holy of holies. the ark of the covenant, the selection of the levitical priests, their holy garments, the consecration and the details of the garments, the ephod the breastplate, the urim and the thummim, the robe, the holy crown, and the mitre. (Exodus 24:12-29:7). "And then in Exodus 29:7, he was appointed to take the anointing oil and put in upon the head of Aaron and his sons. The question again remains, who poured the oil? I ask this question rhetorically, for this Apostolic Father, Moses, poured the oil. He was not a part of the Levitical priesthood; he was an apostolic father to Pharaoh and the nation of Israel.

The Apostle Paul writes in I Corinthians 3:10-11, "According to the grace of God which is given unto me, as a wise master builder, I have laid the foundation, and another buildeth thereon. But let every man take heed, how he buildeth thereupon. For other foundation can no man lay than that is laid, which is Jesus Christ." This is a biblical precept that no other man can alter nor disallow. The Apostle along with his counterpart Silas, a prophet of God, has instituted the Apostolic and Prophetic foundation of the church. It is incumbent on us to understand that it was God's divine plan for Paul and Barnabas to split, thus making a way for the team of Apostle and Prophet to bring forth the Apostolic and Prophetic foundation of the church.

It is our contention that Paul had been prepared from birth, raised up in the city of Tarsus and laid at the feet of the master teacher Gamaliel. He states in Acts 22 that he was taught according to the perfect manner of the law. This Pharisee of

Pharisees was the valedictorian of his time. His knowledge was unprecedented. His manner of life as a Jew was without question. His zeal against the so-called church of Christ was indicative of his knowledge, character, and understanding of Judaism. It's no small wonder that God would select a man skilled in the Judeo principles that would one day bring shadow and form, old and new, together in an eloquence of harmonious bliss, where the very tabernacle of God would find its final resting place within men; that we would become the Ark of the Covenant that would no longer be carried by an ox drawn cart, or carried on the shoulders of the priests, but Christ, the hope of glory would reside within us, the temple of God. Ephesians 2:21-22, "In whom all the building fitly framed together groweth unto an holy temple in the Lord: In whom ye also are builded together for an habitation of God through the Spirit." We as students of God's word must understand that the wise master builder, Paul, who has been selected by God, has become the architect of the church. Matthew 16:18, And I say unto thee, that thou are Peter, and upon this rock of revelation I will build my church; and the gates of hell shall not prevail against it. Upon the revelation of Jesus Christ the church is to be built. Let's get back to the bible . . . I don't need your hermeneutics or your exegetics, I need the Comforter.

Where do we go from here? As we march into the 21st Century, it is imperative that we understand where we are in the total scheme of things, both eternal and temporal. Historically speaking the church has evolved. I call this evolvement the Alpha and Omega concept. The Alpha is a dispensation, the Omega is a dispensation, and there are many dispensations in between. For the gainsayers, let's call these dispensations a paradigm shift, with the understanding that all things are eternal, moving and evolving toward the ultimate purpose. Dominion in the garden, who is in charge? Adam as a steward. The rule and reign of planet earth is the ultimate purpose of the body of Christ. Psalm 110:1-2, "The Lord said unto my Lord, Sit thou at my right hand, until I make thy enemies thy footstool. The Lord shall send the rod of thy strength out of Zion: rule thou in the midst of thine enemies."

We have a very small but essential part to play in the eternal plan of God. There are a few things we need to consider before we can go any further. The scattering of the church, martyrdom of the apostles, the formation of Catholicism, the dark ages, reformation, and the total restoration of the church.

Romans 8:28 reads all things work together for good to them (the body of Christ) who love God and those who are called according to his purpose. It is our job to restore the office of the Apostle and Prophet as the foundation of the church according to Ephesians 2:20, "And are built upon the foundation of the apostles and prophets, Jesus Christ himself being the chief cornerstone." Nowhere in the Word of God does it say that the church is built upon the foundation of the Bishops. As I proceed, do not forget Romans 8:28. **I refer to the Bishops as the surrogate fathers of the church**; or for the gainsayers, once again they are simply out of position. The office of Bishop can be defined as administrative, helps, and/or government. All can be found in I Corinthians 12:5 and there are different administrations but the same Lord. I Corinthians 12:28, "And God hath set some in the church, first apostles, secondarily prophets, thirdly teachers, after that miracles, then gifts of healing, helps, governments, diversities of tongues."

But the Roman Catholic Church has set the Bishop in some Utopian order due to the leftover forms of idolatry that still plagues the church today. It is essential that we complete the Reformation process. The Prophet must come forward and root out, pull down, and destroy those bastions of power, where some even have the audacity in some circles to call Bishops, your grace—No, wrong answer. The Word of God says in Ephesians 2:8, For by grace you are saved through faith; and not of yourself! It is the gift of God.

Historically speaking, this paradox and misuse of the office of Bishop came about during the formation of Catholicism. The Apostle Paul warns the church in Galatians 3:1, "O foolish Galatians, who hath bewitched you, that you should not obey the truth . . ." As Judaism started systematically spreading throughout the church, along with idolatry, thus Catholicism began. Fox's Book of Martyrs details the destruction of the apostles and many spirit-filled believers as the church entered the dark ages, and the emergence of the Catholic godhead, Pope, Archbishops, Bishops, Cardinals, and Priests; and the demise of the Fivefold Ministry. When the reformation began, Martin Luther, as a prophet, pointed the way. We are just completing the process, the ultimate purpose. For example, at the demise of King Saul (religion), the twelve tribes started marching toward Hebron to proclaim David king. So shall we march toward Zion and await our head. Ephesians 5:23, "For the husband is the head of the wife even as Christ is the head of the church: And he is the savior of the body." Verse 27, "That he might present it to himself a glorious church, not having spot, or wrinkle, or any such thing; but that it should be holy and without blemish." From the beginning he has been developing his body.

Matthew 8:20, "And Jesus saith unto him, The foxes have holes, and the birds of the air have nests; but the Son of man hath not where to lay his head." Some of us have no understanding of the completeness of Christ, we see him only as our Savior. We need to understand his Lordship and submit totally to His complete rule and reign as King and High Priest over the church, the body of Christ. When he stated that foxes have holes and birds have nests, but the Son of Man has nowhere to lay his head, he was not speaking about some house, apartment building, or a condo. He speaks of you, the body of Christ, not a paraplegic body, but a body that would not break ranks. When He ascended up on high, His full intent was to come back and gather the body, called Christ. Once again, I reiterate Ephesians 4:12-13, "For the perfecting of the saints, for the work of the ministry, for the edifying of the body of Christ: till we all come in the unity of the faith, and of the knowledge of the Son of God, unto a perfect man, unto the measure of the stature of the fullness of Christ." In these two verses of Scripture we understand that Jesus Christ is head of the church, and we are the body of Christ being perfected by the fivefold ministry, the apostle being the wise master builder, that will bring this body into the measure of the stature of the fullness of Christ. Then the head, Christ, will be able to complete the process of being head of the church. I further reiterate what in Ephesians 1:21-23 says, Christ Jesus was set "far above all principality, and power, and might, and dominion, and every name that is named, not only in this world, but also in that which is to come: And hath put all things under his feet and gave him to be the head over all things to the church, which is his body, the fullness of him that filleth all in all," that you may understand that until we unify and come together as a body, he has nowhere to lay his head—hum—one more time, until we unify and come together as a body, he has nowhere to lay his head.

Joel 2:7 states, "They shall run like mighty men; they shall climb the wall like men of war; and they shall march everyone on his ways, and they shall not break their ranks." Yes, He was preparing his bride. Even then he tells his young disciple to let the dead bury the dead, but you follow me; get your priorities straightened out. When Jesus our head speaks, we are to obey without question.

Romans 8:14, "For as many as are led by the Spirit of God, they are the sons of God." It is time for Sonship ministry, a place where we are totally submitted to the headship of our Lord Jesus, who has been given complete authority to rule and reign in this earthen vessel. Thus, crucifying the flesh, we become dead men as we dare to utter from the rock of Gethsemane those immortal words, not my will, but your will be done.

As free moral agents we have the right to surrender to the Holy Ghost. The whole world is waiting on the manifestation of the sons of God. The Sonship ministry is a place where we become heirs and joint heirs, according to Galatians 4:7, which states, "Wherefore, thou art no more a servant, but a son; and if a son, then an heir of God through Christ." This is the secret place spoken of by King David in shadow form saying, "He that dwelleth in the secret place of the Most High shall abide under the shadow of the Almighty. (Psalm 91:1). Now that is heavy within itself, but no longer do we have only the ability to abide (abide being the key) under the shadow, but the form says, Christ in you, the hope of glory. (Colossians 1:27). John 14:16-17, "And I will pray the Father, and he shall give you another Comforter, that he may abide with you forever; even the Spirit of truth; whom the world cannot receive, because it seeth him not, neither knoweth him: but ye know him; for He dwelleth with you, and shall be in you." Will you now let Him lead you with power and authority as sons of God?

Titus was ordained the first bishop of the church at Crete from Nicopolis to Macedonia. As the Apostle Paul is sent to Rome by King Agrippa, his journey takes him from Caesarea to Tyra and onto Fair Haven, the island of Crete, where Titus was left to set the church in order, Titus 1:5, "For this cause left I thee in Crete, that thou shouldest set in order the things that are wanting, and ordain elders in every city, as I had appointed thee."

It is interesting to note that Titus was not elected by a council of Bishops, or a presbytery, but he was appointed by the Apostle Paul. In the first chapter, he also stated that Titus should set in order the things that are wanting—to exhort and convince the gainsayers and to rebuke false teachers. In Chapter 3:12-13, "When I shall send Artemas unto thee, or Tychicus, be diligent to come unto me to Nicopolis: for I have determined there to winter. Bring Zenas the lawyer and Apollos on their journey diligently, that nothing be wanting unto them." Paul further admonishes this Bishop that is under him to make sure he comes to Nicopolis and brings the lawyer and Apollos with him, and to make sure that all their needs are met. It is our contention that Titus as Bishop has become an administrator. His function is solely to carry out mandates of the apostolic order.

Furthermore we contend that when it speaks of bishopric, it is merely speaking of his duty, his function as treasurer. In the book of Acts 1:20, "For it is written in the book of Psalms, let his habitation be desolate, and let no man dwell therein, and his bishopric let another take." In Acts 1:15-20, they are deciding upon an apostolic appointment: Verse 23, and they appointed two, Justus and Matthias. Verse 25, it reads that they may take part of this ministry and Apostleship. Bishopric is merely his function and his duty as treasurer, an administrator of finances.

In Apostle Paul's first letter to Timothy in Chapter 2:1, it gives the criteria for the office of Bishops and Deacons, almost in the same breath. We have learned in the book of Acts that the Deacons were first appointed because there arose a murmuring of the Grecians against Hebrews. The apostles were starting to be burdened down with settling disputes and making distributions according to each one's needs. The apostle, or Dr. Luke, records in Acts 6:1, "and in those days when the number of disciples were multiplied, there arose a murmuring of the Grecians against the Hebrews, because their widows were neglected in the daily ministration. The word "ministration" (Webster's New World Dictionary) is defined as the act of giving help or cares; service. They became distributors of provision.

As we further examine I Timothy 3, I pose the question: Why are the qualifications for Bishops and Deacons strikingly similar? It is as if there is a job opening, and these are the qualifications for employment. It's not a calling, nor an election. It is merely an appointment according to these guidelines. The Bishop's duty is mainly administrative on a larger scale. They are to keep the provisions that have been laid at the apostles' feet flowing, while the apostles give themselves to prayer and the Word.

This doctrinal error has caused the death and the destruction of the very bedrock of the church. It's no wonder the people are perishing for a lack of knowledge. They do not understand nor respect the foundational offices of Apostle and Prophet because of the Utopian vanguard that has received its doctrine from Catholicism in error, which promoted the very demigod that represents the one world church. This same system of error plunged the so-called church into a dark age. The blood of the martyred is still crying out under the throne room of God. How long? But alas, this same system of Bishops has diluted the power and authority of God's headship of Apostles and Prophets long enough.

Even in the distance I hear the drumbeat, I see the writing on the wall, while the band is playing the number one gospel track. There is a paradigm shifting, while those men of renown have been caught in an identity crises, clamoring to get on the bandwagon. I've often heard an off-the-cuff prose such as, I thought you knew the council elected me as a Bishop, but I am an Apostle. As the day dawns, the curtain closes and the paradigm begins its final descent as they continue to adorn themselves with the miter, the robe, the ring, the cross, and staff of Bishop or Archbishop. By the sleight of hand as a magician pulls a rabbit out of his hat or a dove appears from nowhere,

I can hear them say in the middle of this dispensational shift, I was always an apostle or prophet. Did you not know? (Smile.)

It's really okay. We must understand that many of these enshrouded in the office of Bishop were called to be Apostles and Prophets, but because of the fear of persecution they hid. Bishop Earl Paulk is a true Prophet of God. I know him by his fruit; he is the one that God chose to point Kingdom direction while it was yet unpopular. His stand on the Kingdom of God caused him to be almost destroyed, but he stood. And now everyone is starting to preach on the Kingdom of God from the revelation that God gave him only a few years ago. He was the vessel that God flowed this powerful revelation through. As a forerunner, this Prophet begins to unfold the mystery of the Kingdom of God, not the Late Great Planet Earth. That is a totally ridiculous concept.

While recently in Liberia, West Africa, in the city of Kakata about an hour from Monrovia, I installed the first Bishop of that city, a son under this apostolic mantle. Bishop Emmanuel Sesay heads at this time four branches of the Kingdom Of God Apostolic and Prophetic Ministries International (KOGAPMI). He, as the National Director of Liberia, West Africa, understands the order of Bishop under the apostle and fathering spirit. We will begin to see unprecedented miracles, growth, and development for that area as the foundation of the church has been reestablished in divine order . . . Today, December 12, 2012, there are now 10 branches in which this spiritual son oversees KOGAPMI under apostolic order.

If you would now turn to your New Strong's Exhaustive Concordance of the Bible, I would like for you, the student reader, to look up the word "Bishop." It appears six times as Bishop, one time as Bishopricks, and one time as Bishops (plural), a total of eight times. The word "Apostle" is written 19 times singular, 57 times in plural form, and a total of 82 times in one form or another.

I Timothy 3:1, "This is a true saying, If a man desire the office of a **bishop**, he desireth a good work."

I Timothy 3:2, "A **bishop** then must be blameless, the husband of one wife, vigilant, sober, of good behavior, given to hospitality, apt to teach."

II Timothy 4:22, "The Lord Jesus Christ be with thy spirit. Grace be with you. Amen." [The second epistle unto Timotheus, ordained the first **bishop** of the church of the Ephesians, was written from Rome, when Paul was brought before Nero the second time.]

Titus 1:7, "For a **bishop** must be blameless, as the steward of God; not selfwilled, not soon angry, not given to wine, no striker, not given to filthy lucre."

Titus 3:15, "All that are with me salute thee. Greet them that love us in the faith. Grace be with you all. Amen." [It was written to Titus, ordained the first **bishop** of the church of the Cretians, from Nicopolis in Macedonia.]

I Peter 2:25, "For ye were as sheep going astray; but are now returned unto the Shepherd and **Bishop** of your souls."

Acts 1:20, "For it is written in the book of Psalms, Let his habitation be desolate, and let no man dwell therein: and his **bishoprick** let another take.

Philippians 1:1, "Paul and Timotheus, the servants of Jesus Christ, to all the saints in Christ Jesus which are at Philippi, with the **bishops** and deacons."

Last but not least in Philippians 3:17 the Apostle Paul admonishes the **bishops** and deacons through his epistle, which says, "Brethren, be followers together of me . . ."

Prophetic Headline: Word of prophecy from the Apostle:

Beware of the bishops' 21st Century move to a monarchial structure in America's mainstream denominations. Again, you cannot put new wine in old wine skins.

Apostle M.S. Sterling

Chapter 8

A WISE MASTER BUILDER

The Wise Master Builder—I Corinthians 3:10-11, "According to the grace of God which is given unto me, as a wise master builder, I have laid the foundation, and another buildeth thereon. But let every man take heed how he buildeth thereupon. For other foundation can no man lay than that is laid, which is Jesus Christ."

This is a precept and a safeguard that was to guard against sectarianism. Paul had previously stated when partyism had arisen in the church where one would say I am of Paul, another I am of Apollos, and still yet another stated I am of Cephas—he stated that they were babes. Down history's lane they now say, I am of Baptist persuasion, or I am of Pentecostal persuasion, or one of the many other denominational sects. The Apostle Paul stated, I planted, Apollos watered, but it was God that gave the increase. The wise master builder, Paul, had built a foundational church that would remain as one organism with many cells;

that is, one body with different members and functions, but one united source. Paul, the Apostle, and Silas, the Prophet, became the foundation of the church with Christ as the chief cornerstone.

He warned them to be careful how they built thereupon, whether it were of gold, silver, precious stones, wood, hay, or stubble. There would come a time of testing and every man's work would be tested as if by fire. Has this sectarian church been tested by fire? I say not. But judgment shall begin in the house of God (I Peter 4:17).

My question to you, the reader is: Are you upon a sure foundation according to the Word of God? What is your Bishop or Pastor saying? Is your church or your denomination the only way? This is a sure sign of a shaky foundation that will not stand the test of fire. You might pose the question: Well our denomination has been here 150 years? That is just a small time with God. The children of Israel were in Egypt 400 years before God brought Egypt to its knees. So please do not base your self-examinations on a minute time slot. It's time to get back to the basics. The sure foundation of the Word of God clearly states in Ephesians 2:19-20, "Now therefore ye are no more strangers and foreigners, but fellow citizens with the saints, and of the household of God; and are built upon the foundation of the apostles and prophets, Jesus Christ himself being the chief cornerstone."

Now for all of you mythology teachers, who say there are no longer Apostles and Prophets, you are liars, deceivers and perverts of God's Word. You belong to the church of the frozen chosen. You are among the walking dead; you have a form of godliness, but are denying the power thereof. You would not know revelation if it bit you. Most likely you are still relying on the stale manna that the founder of your denomination gave 150 years ago.

Many of the old hardliners say that the apostles were those who walked with Jesus. Well, Paul did not walk with Jesus in the natural, but had a spiritual awakening on the way to Damascus. He met Jesus in spirit. For the Word says that he heard a voice, but saw no man (Acts 9:8). What about Barnabas in Acts 14:14?

So if Paul never walked with Jesus, but had a spiritual encounter when he talked to Him, can this not still happen today? I say yes, because it happened to me in Nigeria, West Africa, July 24, 2000. I had been going forward in my calling as an apostle for a few years, knowing that my commission was coming. It came that night right after 6 o'clock in-the-morning intercession. I was lying on top of the bed meditating on the Word, when He entered my room. My eyes were closed and I

DR. MICHAEL P. STERLING

was determined not to be afraid. I said rhetorically, if it is you, Lord, touch me. Oh and He touched me with a physical touch that went from my head throughout my entire being. That day I was fully commissioned as an Apostle of the most High God.

The Word of God clearly states in Ephesians 4:11-14, "And he gave some apostles, and some prophets; and some evangelists; and some pastors and teachers; for the perfecting of the saints, for the work of the ministry, for the edifying of the body of Christ." Now the next verse is the key: "Till we all come in the unity of the faith, and of the knowledge of the Son of God, unto a perfect man, unto the measure of the stature of the fullness of Christ."

Now Readers, ask yourselves this simple question: Have we all come together in the unity of the faith? The answer is emphatically no! Paul, the wise master builder, clearly states, that the Fivefold ministry was to perfect the saints until we all come into the unity of the faith. We are not there; we are a divided nation or a divided church.

Let's throw the babe out with the bath water. For this religious baby has grown up to be a full-grown monster. Our only saving grace is the Word of God.

Romans 8:28 reads, all things work together for the good for those who love the Lord and those who are called according to his purpose. So the reformation process is still going forward. It has been God's perfect plan. I was being somewhat crude, to provoke you. It's time for an awakening; it's time to mature in the measure of the stature of the fullness of Christ. It's time to grow up, Church. I charge you, come out from among them. I Corinthians 13:11, "When I was a child, I spake as a child, I understood as a child, I thought as a child; but when I became a man, I put away childish things." We must move on into spiritual maturity. I Peter 2:5, "Ye also, as lively stones, are built up a spiritual house, an holy priesthood, to offer up spiritual sacrifices, acceptable to God by Jesus Christ." Each one of us must become a living stone, holy and acceptable to God. Some must be totally broken and crushed, then grounded to powder and mixed with the pure water of the Word, taken back to the potter's wheel and remodeled or reclassified, then placed in the body, the church, thus becoming fitly framed together for a habitation of God through the spirit. The Apostle Paul says in Ephesians 4:14, "That we henceforth be no more children, tossed to and fro, and carried about with every wind of doctrine." These different doctrines are exactly what he was referring to, the "Club Med Mentality," that has entered certain denominations like a socialite whore, prostituting herself off to those sectarian spirits who remain reclusive by denomination, race, or social status.

These forms of idolatry will no longer be tolerated by the great grace provision of the New Testament Church.

Judgment Shall Begin in the House of God. Your Hour of Visitation Draweth Nigh. Hebrews 12:27-29, "And this word, Yet once more, signifieth the removing of those things that are shaken, as of things that are made, that those things which cannot be shaken may remain." The wise master builder talks about the foundation of the Apostles and Prophets, Jesus Christ being the chief cornerstone. A true Apostle and Prophet of the 21st Century will always point to a united church. They have no hidden agendas. They understand Kingdom precepts. They understand that soon to come upon the church is the test of fire. Verse 29, "For our God is a consuming fire."

As I look back to the beginning of the Reformation, I can almost see a puzzled Martin Luther, who has been awakened to revelation knowledge. This 15th Century Priest was provoked to come out from his denominational sect, thus proclaiming a 95 thesis of doctrinal era and truth. A new dispensation begins, as this snowball begins to slowly roll down the hill, while Martin Luther becomes an outcast and a hunted man. He loses everything and all that he has studied for. His chasten body has been sacrificed on the altar of self-denial. Now, because of this revelation of truth, he was labeled a heretic and an outlaw, but the truth had set him free. This 15th Century Prophet of God has set in motion an eternal reformation that cannot be stopped.

As the Reformation of the church began, the Protestants started their campaign against Catholicism, and this once all powerful church of the one world religion, which has killed and martyred many noble saints of God, now faces her greatest foe, Reformation. This idolatrous monster, the Babylonian whore, for the first time in history begins to show a weakness. This once powerful organization of church and state was instituted by Constantine, the first Roman emperor to become a Christian. He brought forth a freedom of religion act that caused an end to the martyrdom of the faith, but would continue the demise of the fivefold ministry to a form of godliness where the pope hierarchy would bring the government and church into the depth of corruption, along with the counterpart, the Jesuit order. There is now an awakening of the fivefold ministry, and this old order cannot stop this dispensation of truth from shaking the very bedrock of its doctrinal foundation based upon Bishops, Cardinals, Popes, Monks and Priests, idolatry, and a pinch of Judaism. (We still cannot put new wine into old wineskins).

Galatians 3:1, "Oh foolish Galatians, who has bewitched you?" The Apostle Paul had given warning, but alas they did not heed the proclamation of Martin Luther against Catholicism. The

Protestant movement brings about a vigorous campaign against the old order. Next we see a rise of many sectarian movements, such as the Lutherans, the Presbyterians, the hardline Orthodox Church, and many others as the Reformation begins to unfold. Many types of council are formed and various groups assemble. Great men appear on the scene, such as Wesley and Calvin, but where is the wise master builder, one who gathers and does not scatter? The very foundation of the church is missing. So now we find ourselves steeped in sectarianism while the clutches of division, alienation, and seclusion begins to disembody the church. Saints of God, you have been hoodwinked long enough. I know that many of you realize that there is only one church, whose builder and maker is God. Shall you remain loyal to the denomination, or will you demand change. And if they refuse to line up with the Word of God, will you come out from among them? You must find a church that is non-divided, who proclaims the one fold, one shepherd status.

John 10:16, "And other sheep I have, which are not of this fold: Them also must I bring, and they shall hear my voice; and there shall be one fold, and one shepherd."

Do you hear His voice? Come out from among them!

Chapter 9

THE DESIGN OF THE CHURCH

The Church at Jerusalem
Centralized Authority

As we begin to understand the fivefold ministry more clearly, it is necessary that we begin to re-evaluate the design and structure of the church. There is and must be centralized authority as was in the early Jerusalem church, where James, the brother of Jesus, was a type of chief apostle, not a bishop and surely not a Pope, but an apostle. James, as we will read is the centralized authority and has theocratic rule. He was most definitely in charge. In his ruling (Greek krino: for sentence or judgment) we find that he has the final word, and the rest of the apostles, prophets, teachers, and elders lined up with his authority. It is evident that the great Apostle Peter, Paul and the Prophet Silas, understood his authority and submitted wholeheartedly.

The Legislative and Spiritual Authority of the Jerusalem Church.

The presbytery of elders

James, Chief Apostle. Acts 15:19, "Wherefore my sentence is, that we trouble not them, which from among the Gentiles are turned to God."

As we read in Acts 15:1, "And certain men which came down from Judea taught the brethren, and said, Except ye be circumcised after the manner of Moses, ye cannot be saved." These were the same persons mentioned by Paul in Galatians 2:12 who came from James and the Jerusalem church. James was the equivalent of the "leading elder" in Jerusalem, especially influential as the brother of the Lord; and presumably, he was supported, or at least not opposed, by the apostles. These men from James exceeded their commission by thus making observance of the Mosaic Law mandatory for all Christians; and James declared that "no such commandment" was given them (Acts 15:24). He seems, however, to have tolerated their views until this crisis.

It appears at this point that the greatest doctrinal threat in its whole history now confronted the young faith of the new church. In any case, if God had not corrected the apostles and elders in Jerusalem, the entire Christian religion would have been frustrated and perverted. At best, it could thenceforth have been nothing but a Jewish sect, preaching the resurrection of Christ, of course, but nevertheless relying on the Law of Moses for salvation. A large company of Pharisees who had become Christians would soon have dominated and destroyed it. Thus, what is in view here is a very sharp clash between Paul's true position and the false position of the men who had come from Jerusalem. Galatians 2:2 plainly reads that Paul went up by **revelation** and communicated unto them the gospel. It is no doubt that the church did appoint them; but that is not the reason Paul went; the Lord commanded him to go.

It should be noted that Luke carefully refrained from saying that they were to go to Jerusalem to settle the question, leaving in view the fact that through Paul's revelation they were going to settle the question at the Jerusalem church. The stubborn insistence of the Judean emissaries made it clear that some in the Jerusalem church intended to control the churches everywhere, compelling them to conform to their Judaist bias. Thus, in order to root out the heresy, it was necessary that strong action be taken against the source of it in Jerusalem.

Not only had they corrupted practically the whole of the church in Judea, but the recently established churches in Galatia had been visited and corrupted sufficiently to call forth Paul's letter to the Galatians. The representatives they sent up to Antioch probably expected a quick victory there also; but instead of a victory they confronted the dauntless Paul, who challenged them, defeated them, and proceeded to Jerusalem where he reversed the victory they had already won there. Aside from Christ himself, Christianity owes more to Paul than to any other. Now on behalf of the apostolic movement, Acts 15:8-9 reads, "And God who knoweth the heart, bare them witness, giving them the Holy Spirit, even as he did unto us; and he made no distinction between us and them, cleansing their hearts by faith." This is one of the cornerstone doctrines of Christianity. God has one plan, one system of human salvation, there being no partiality, no special favors, no special devices favoring any man, race, or nation. Jews and Gentiles alike confront the same message in Christ. The whole book of Romans was written to develop the theme of God's righteousness in treating all men and nations alike. "There is no distinction!" (Romans 3:22).

This thunderbolt just delivered by Peter completely silenced the Pharisaical Christianity Party, leaving the vast body of the Jerusalem church, assembled for the occasion, silent and ready to give full attention to the report of Barnabas and Paul. In this Jerusalem situation, Luke returned to the old order of these names. That report included all that Luke recorded in the last two chapters preceding this, and possibly a great deal more, proving beyond question of doubt, that the hand of the Lord was with Paul and Barnabas on that journey, and by implication, proving Pauline teaching to be God's truth. Before the conference a complete settlement was reached. The twelve acknowledged Paul's teaching as orthodox, recognized him as the apostle to the Gentiles, conceded his demand that the Gentiles should be free from the observance of the law, and gave him the right hand of fellowship. After this, the result of the Council was a foregone conclusion. Acts 15:19, "Wherefore my sentence is that we trouble not them, which from among the Gentiles are turned to God." James here did not announce the findings of the council but his own judgment. The four prohibitions here that the Christians should refrain from: (1) pollutions of idols, (2) fornication, (3) things strangled, and (4) blood. The binding nature of these restrictions was pointed out by root. Not only the apostles and elders and brethren, but also the Holy Spirit concurred in the message (Acts 15:28), making this an inspired message, not merely a ruling of the church or its leaders.

"Then it seemed good to the apostles and elders, with the whole church, to send chosen men of their own company to Antioch with Paul and Barnabas; namely, Judas called Barsabas, and Silas, chief men among the brethren." Acts: 15:22. The wise precaution observed here was that of providing a dual witness with the representatives of both sides, in order to forestall any recurrence of disunity. Silas, the same as Silvanus, may have been met here for the first time by Paul, marking the beginning of a relationship that was to continue on the mission field. Silas would prove an invaluable ally for Paul; because, coming from Jerusalem, he would be able to verify the recognition of Paul's apostleship by the whole church. "So when they were dismissed, came to Antioch; and when they had gathered the multitude together, they delivered the epistle: Which when they had read, they rejoiced for the consolation." (Acts 15: 30-31).

"And after they had tarried there a space, they were let go in peace from the brethren unto the apostles" (Acts 15:33). "And some days after Paul said unto Barnabas, Let us go again and visit our brethren in every city where we have preached the word of the Lord, and see how they do" (Acts 15:36). Paul was very diligent to keep on teaching in order to prevent discouragement and defection.

It would appear that he had every intention of making the excursion with Barnabas until Barnabas insisted on taking his nephew, John Mark. "But Paul thought not good to take him with them, who departed from them from Pamphylia, and went not with them to the work. And the contention was so sharp between them, that they parted asunder one from the other: and so Barnabas took Mark, and sailed unto Cyprus" (Acts 15:38-39).

Strong men with minds strongly made up often find disagreement between them; and the one redeeming note in this otherwise unhappy and regrettable episode is that neither party to the dispute permitted it to hinder the work of God. Rather there was beneficial result in that there were then two teams of missionaries on the field in the place of only one. It was but natural that Barnabas would prefer the journey to his native Cyprus. Dr. Luke would record most of the acts of the Apostles, especially the missionaries journeys of Paul.

In the apostolic and prophetic movement there must be a centralized authority that will lend credence to the vineyard as a whole. Several years ago a great apostle proposed an International Congress of Apostles and Prophets. A powerful prophet brought this vision to me. I ran with it. The very first year was awesome as apostles and prophets began to gather from all over the country and other parts of the world. It was almost destroyed by an apostle, who I considered my father in the Lord. God saw fit to take him home. Let's finish the work . . . calling all apostles and prophets for the 2013 International Congress of Apostles and Prophets. There is centralized authority in the COGIC with Bishop G.E. Patterson. There is centralized authority in the Assemblies of God, Southern Baptist, and Word of Faith. It is time for us, the apostles and prophets of the apostolic and prophetic, to come together as one, then extend a hand to the body of Christ and prepare the Bride of Christ for the second coming. Revelation 19:7, "Let us be glad and rejoice, and give honor to Him: for the marriage of the Lamb is come, and his wife hath made herself ready." Yes! We have to prepare the Bride. It's not going to happen by itself. It's incumbent upon us, the end-time generals, leaders, apostles, prophets, and fivefold ministers to understand apostolic revelation.

Apostolic & Prophetic Revelation

Ephesians 3:2-5, "If ye have heard of the dispensation of the grace of God, which is given me to you ward: How that by revelation he made known unto me the mystery; (as I wrote afore in few words, Whereby, when ye read, ye may understand my knowledge in the mystery of Christ) Which in other ages was not made known unto the sons of men, as it is now revealed unto his holy apostles and prophets by the Spirit."

Matthew 16:17, "And Jesus answered and said unto him, Blessed art thou, Simon Barjona: for flesh and blood hath not revealed it unto thee, but my Father which is in heaven."

I Corinthians 2:10, "But God hath revealed them unto us by his Spirit, for the Spirit searches all things, yea, the deep things of God."

Amos 3:7, "Surely the Lord God will do nothing, but he revealeth his secret unto his servants the prophets."

II Corinthians 12:1, "It is not expedient for me doubtless to glory. I will come to visions and revelations of the Lord."

II Corinthians 12:7, "And lest I should be exalted above measure through the abundance of revelations, there was given to men then in the flesh, the messenger of Satan to buffet me, lest I should be exalted above measure."

Church Government

Increase / constant / perpetual

Isaiah 9:6

"Government"

Increase of His government,

Apostles and Prophets,

Government was on the

Shoulders of Christ. (Isaiah 22:22)

Ephesians 2:20

"Foundation"

of Apostles and Prophets

to the chief cornerstone

Built on Revelation

Matthew 16:18

"Church"

Rock/revelation

Apostle Peter received

Revelation through the

Holy Spirit

I Corinthians 3:10

"Builder"

This is the Apostle Paul

He was an architect and

master builder of the church.

Pattern—The Design of the Church.

Hebrews 8:5, "Who serve unto the example and shadow of heavenly things, as Moses was admonished of God when he was about to make the tabernacle: for, See, saith he, that thou make all things according to the pattern shewed to thee in the mount." Ephesians 4:11 . . . I Corinthians 12:28 . . . this is the pattern . . . I Corinthians 3:10 . . . this is the pattern . . . Ephesians 2:20-22 . . . this is the pattern . . . Matthew 16:18 . . . this is the pattern . . . Revelation 21:14.

When we talk about Fivefold Ministry, it is essential that we begin to understand that God is the potter and we are merely clay. He has invested his authority in this delegation of ministry gifts, Ephesians 4:8, "And he gave gifts unto men." Ephesians 4:11-13 sates clearly, "And he gave some apostles; and some, prophets; and some, evangelists; and some, pastors and teachers; For the perfecting of the saints, for the working of the ministry, for the edifying of the body of Christ . . . till we all come into the unity of the faith and the knowledge of the Son of God unto a perfect man, unto the measure of stature of the fullness of Christ." Understanding Ephesians 4:11 is a tall order and has been looked over, misunderstood, and literally rejected. Let's begin to dissect these verses of scriptures and get a clear view of our duties as fivefold ministry gifts to God.

1. To perfect the saints
2. For the work of the ministry
3. For the edifying of the body
4. Until we all come into the unity of the faith
5. Unto knowledge of the Son of God
6. Unto a perfect man
7. Stature of the fullness of Christ.

Ephesians 4:12

1. For the perfecting of the saints . . . ongoing process . . . root word perfect (Webster's) = complete in all respects, without defect, flawless
2. For the work of the ministry . . . the saints are supposed to do the work.
3. For the edifying of the body of Christ
4. Ephesians 4:13 till—until. Up to the time of . . . till (a specific time or occurrence) we all come into the unity of the faith?

5. And unto the knowledge of the Son of God . . . knowledge. The act, fact or state of knowing.

6. Unto a perfect man . . . perfect, flawless.

7. Unto the measure of the stature of the fullness of Christ.

1. Measure—Greek Metron = limited portion degree

2. Stature—Greek Helikia = maturity

3. Fullness—Greek Pleroma—repletion or completion, what is put in to fill up, fulfilling, full, fullness

Let us examine I Corinthians 3 as we begin to close this chapter. The Apostle Paul clearly states here, verse 6, "I have planted, Apollos watered; but God gave the increase. So then neither is he that planted anything, neither he that watered; but God that giveth the increase." Verse 9, "For we are laborers together with God: Ye are God's husbandry, ye are God's building. Now verse 10 is the kicker: When we begin to look at the church spiritually and not carnally. For example, imagine it like this: God has a vision for a city, a nation, or in actuality a church. He comes out of heaven and begins to gather 12 pillars or 12 foundations as stated in Revelation 21:14, "And the wall of the city had twelve foundations, and in them the names of the twelve apostles of the Lamb." Paul is not mentioned here, for he is an ascension apostle. Now Jesus, as He was walking, begins to ask a question of the twelve as mentioned in Matthew Chapter 16:13. He spoke to the clay that the potter was molding (in disciple form). "Whom do men say that I the Son of Man am?" The majority began to say, verse 14, "And they said, Some say that thou art John the Baptist, some Elias and others Jeremiah, or one of the prophets."

Jesus says more or less okay! That's what you heard, but whom say ye that I am? Simon Peter who begins to have revelation; says you are the Christ the Son of the living God. Now for the first time in history the word church is spoken into existence. As Jesus replies upon this Rock I will build my church and the gates of hell will not prevail against it, the door to the Kingdom has been eternally opened, and Peter is given the key, not yet realizing the fullness of a new dispensation coming into view. This disciple will continue to go through the fire of carnality as the dross of flesh is burned away. He will deny this very same Christ three times and will be found in a backslidden condition.

After the resurrection of Jesus, who would walk among men for over 40 days, and would find Peter at the sea of Tiberius. This Peter with the sons of Zebedee, James and John, along with the great apostle Paul will one day line up with the authority of the Jerusalem Church, each having various ministries. But in the final analysis, they submit to James, the brother of Jesus, who has taken a Nazarite vow, who heads the church at Jerusalem, which will become the center of authority. The Apostle Paul, who became the architect of the church, states in I Corinthians 3:10, "According to the grace of God which is given unto me, as a wise master builder, I have laid the foundation, and another built thereon. But let every man take heed how he buildeth thereupon." The question is: Have you taken heed? Or are you bound by tradition?

The Six Doctrinal Principles of Christ—The Seventh Perfection Apostles Doctrine (Acts 2:42).

Hebrews 6:1, "Therefore, leaving the principles of the doctrine of Christ, let us go on unto perfection; not laying again the foundation of repentance from dead works, and faith towards God, of the doctrine of baptisms, and of laying on of hands, and of resurrection of the dead, and of eternal judgment." Here you will find the six doctrinal principles of Christ, the seventh being perfection.

The Apostle Paul admonishes the church in Hebrews 5:12, "For when for the time ye ought to be teachers, ye have need that one teach you again which be the first principles of the oracles of God; and are become such as have need of milk, and not of strong meat."

Principles

1. Repentance
2. Faith toward God
3. Baptisms
4. Laying on of hands
5. Resurrection of the dead
6. Eternal judgment

Repentance

Matthew 3:2, ". . . and saying repent ye; for the Kingdom of Heaven is at hand."

Matthew 4:17, "From that time Jesus began to preach, and to say, Repent: for the Kingdom of heaven is at hand.
Acts 2:38, " . . . then Peter said unto them repent."

Faith

Hebrews 11:1, "Now faith is the substance of things hoped for and the evidence of things not seen."

Hebrews 11:6, "but without faith it is impossible to please God."

Baptisms

John 3:5, ". . . Jesus answered, verily, verily I say unto thee, except a man be born of water and of the spirit, he cannot enter the Kingdom of God."

Matthew 28:19, "Go ye therefore and teach all nations, baptizing them in the name of the Father, and of the Son, and of the Holy Ghost."

Acts 2:38, "Then Peter said unto them, Repent, and be baptized every one of you in the name of Jesus Christ for the remission of sins and ye shall receive the gift of the Holy Ghost.

Acts 4:7, "By what power, of by what name have you done this?"

Acts 4:12, "Neither is there salvation in any other; for there is none other name under heaven given among men, whereby we must be saved."

Ephesians 4:5, "one Lord, one faith, one baptism.

Laying on of Hands

Acts 8:17, "Then laid their hands on them, and they received the Holy Ghost."

II Timothy 1:6, "Wherefore I put thou in remembrance that thou stir up the gift of God, which is in thee by the putting on of my hands."

Romans 8:1, "For I long to see you that I might impart some spiritual gift unto you to the end ye may be established."

Resurrection of the Dead—(Pharisees believe in the resurrection). I Corinthians 15:14, "And if Christ be not risen, then is our preaching vain, and your faith is also vain."

John 11:25, "Jesus said unto her, I am the resurrection, and the life: He that believeth in me, though he were dead, yet shall he live."

Eternal Judgment

Hebrews 9:27, "And it is appointed unto men once to die, but after this the judgment."

Psalm 1:5, "Therefore the ungodly shall not stand in the judgment, nor the sinners in the congregation of the righteous." Acts 2:42, "And they continued steadfast in the apostles' doctrine and fellowship and in breaking of bread and in prayers."

Finally in Hebrews 5:12, the Bible says, "For when for the time ye ought to be teachers, ye have need that one teach you again which be the first principles of the oracles of God; and are become such as have need of milk, and not of strong meat."

Building the body is our mission. Perfection is our statement. Maturity is our goal and fullness is when He will come for a church without spot, wrinkle or blemish.

Chapter 10

THE KINGDOM AND
THE CHURCH

To understand the universal kingdom first and foremost it has always been about the kingdom, and it will always be about the kingdom and its sovereign king and its LORD Elohim, who is omnipotent, omnipresent, and omniscient. He as God ruled over all things, created all things, and is everywhere at the same time. He sits in heaven as God and came to earth as God the Son, Christ Jesus, who while in heaven walked in the earth. We now understand that he is and always will be one, Father, Son, and Holy Spirit. We can also clearly find this stated in Isaiah 6:8, when he said, "Also I heard the voice of the Lord, saying, Whom shall I send, and who will go for **us**? Then said I, Here am I; send me." The word "us" has been emphasized to show the Elohim/ Adonai relationship (Psalm 110:1). The Word of God says in the book of John 1:1-3, "In the beginning was the Word, and the Word was with God, and the Word was God. The same was in the beginning with God. All things were made by him; and without him was not anything made that was made."

God in the beginning of our world created man in His image and likeness. So then before the fall, man was like god and was given full authority to act on his behalf in the earth realm. He was given dominion according to Genesis 1:26. He created man with a dual nature, male and female. In Genesis 2:21-23, he took the dual nature out of man by way of his rib and created woman. This woman was supposed to be the helpmeet according to Genesis 2:20. They were to rule in the Kingdom of God, not in the Kingdom of Heaven, which is God's dominion alone. Their assignment was to be fruitful and multiply after the image and likeness of God. When man fell he lost the **image** of God, but maintained His likeness. We as biblical scholars believe this image that was lost was the essence of God's glory. This is why man, Adam, found himself naked outside the image, the very covering of glory.

It is evident that now God has a problem, (or should I say, Houston, there is a problem.) Here fallen man is inside of paradise, the garden, where there are two eternal trees, the Tree of the Knowledge of Good and Evil which man has already eaten, and the Tree of Life, which if he eats he will live forever in this fallen state. So now God must exile man from the garden, then place the Cherubim angels with a flaming sword, which turned every way, to keep man from the Tree of Life. Then fallen man goes from bad to worse as the earth population begins to increase. God's purpose and plan for the earth has been altered but has not changed. He must put in motion a plan of restoration and redemption that would take centuries to fulfill. First, he must cleanse the whole earth with a flood, save one man and his family which consists of eight souls. I want you, the reader, to understand that **God must take or use imperfect man to fulfill His perfect plan**. The Bible says in Genesis 6:9, "These are the generations of Noah, Noah was a just man and perfect is his generations, and Noah walked with God." Through Noah's obedience his wife, three sons, and their three wives were saved, a total of eight people, which represents a new beginning. The process of redemption, the continuation of man, from Noah to Abraham spanned many earthly years. Phase 2, so now God must choose a man, Abram, who would obey His command and separate himself from family and friends. He would become the father of many nations, our Father Abraham, and his lineage would become the nation of Israel—from Abraham, who symbolizes the legacy, to Isaac, who received the heritage, to Jacob, who is now the blessed one, whose seed we now know as the twelve tribes of Israel. We must understand that our bible and its sacred writings are types and shadows of events that are occurring over and over again with the same intent and purpose—the restoration process of mankind.

Definition of Restoration (Dictionary.com)

1. The act of restoring, renewal, revival, or reestablishment.
2. The state of fact of being restored.
3. A return of something to a former, original, normal, or unimpaired condition.

So now we have Noah in process who was found drunk and naked, and Abraham who gets ahead of God and creates an Ishmael, while yet Isaac, the promise, is on the way. And what about Moses, the law giver, who hits the rock instead of following the instructions to speak to the rock, which cost him his promise land experience? When we really begin to understand in the redemptive process God has used imperfect man to create a vehicle and a legal highway by which he can step out of heaven, become a seed in a young virgin girl named Mary, while ultimately becoming the sacrificial Lamb for all mankind. Hebrews 9:22 says, "And almost all things are by the law purged with blood; and without shedding of blood is no remission." In Isaiah 7:14, the prophet Isaiah prophecies the coming Messiah, "Therefore the Lord himself shall give you a sign; Behold, a virgin shall conceive, and bear a son, and shall call his name Immanuel." This Immanuel, God with us, Jesus the Christ would open a new door by which man can be restored. This door is called the church.

The Church, The Backup Plan

The church has become God's backup plan for man's ultimate transformation (back to the future) or should I say back to the beginning when man possessed the image and likeness of God. In the born again application man can once again see the Kingdom of God and can enter in through its doors. The Bible says in John 3:3-5, "Jesus answered and said unto him, Verily, verily, I say unto thee, Except a man be born again, he cannot see the kingdom of God. Nicodemus saith unto him, How can a man be born when he is old? Can he enter the second time into his mother's womb, and be born? Jesus answered, Verily, verily, I say unto thee, Except a man be born of water and of the Spirit, he cannot enter into the kingdom of God."

Wow, what a plan! When a sinner goes down and is baptized he is baptized into the death of Christ, which is symbolic of the grave. When he comes up from the water the old nature is gone and the new life begins. He is baptized in the spirit and is born again, thus having a new lease on life. In this process of death, burial, and resurrection man is now continuing the process of restoration by the renewing of his mind. 2 Corinthians 5:17, "Therefore if any man be in Christ, he is a new creature: old things are passed away; behold, all things are become new." There is still more process to the ultimate transformation of mankind back to the image of God.

The Bible and its 66 books is the ultimate restoration plan of God. Throughout the Scriptures Jesus, the Word, seeks to save that which is lost. As in the book of Romans Chapter 8:28-30, it reads, "And we know that all things work together for good to them that love God, to them who are the called according to his purpose. For whom he did foreknow, he also did predestinate to be conformed to the **image** of his Son, that he might be the firstborn among many brethren. Moreover whom he did predestinate, them he also called: and whom he called, them he also justified: and whom he justified, them he also glorified." Here we find the word "image" once again, that those predestinated would be conformed to the image of his Son (back to the future). The glory which was lost in the garden is the very image of God, the chief cornerstone or the Holy Spirit is working on the inside of each living stone through conviction of conscience by the word of God. Mankind is being built and prepared as a mansion of God. The wise master builders, the apostles along with the prophets, evangelists, pastors and teachers are perfecting the saints.

The church or ecclesia are the called out ones, the true church of the living God. You see we are not speaking of natural brick or mortar as in a cathedral or edifice. This church, temple of God, is a fully functioning mobile unit that houses the very essence of God. Let's go back and evaluate I Corinthians 3:16-17, "Know ye not that ye are the temple of God, and that the Spirit of God dwelleth in you? If any man defile the temple of God, him shall God destroy; for the temple of God is holy, which temple ye are."

So now you, the church, have been given the keys to the kingdom by the same revelation that the Apostle Peter had through divine revelation that Jesus is and was the Christ, the Son of the Living God. Not only do you have the keys to the kingdom, you have been baptized into the new birth. This is why we believe that total submission is essential, because the baptismal pool becomes your grave or coffin. When one is baptized he dies from the old nature, old things are passed away. Behold all things become new. In Hebrews 6:2 it speaks of the doctrine of baptisms. The word baptisms is plural. But in some cases there has only been the baptism of water unto salvation. But the second is the baptism of fire, which should be experienced all at once. But due to the predilections of men, many have been baptized unto salvation but not unto the power of the Holy Spirit. It is my belief that they will reach heaven, but will walk as second class citizens in the earth realm.

When Jesus spoke to Nicodemus he explained unto him the kingdom of God (John 3:3-5). "Jesus answered and said unto him, Verily, verily, I say unto thee, Except a man be born again, he cannot see the kingdom of God. Nicodemus saith unto him, How can a man be born when he is old? Can he enter the second time into his mother's womb, and be born? Jesus answered, Verily, verily, I say unto thee, Except a man be born of water and of the Spirit, he cannot enter into the kingdom of God?" This is and should always be a dual operation. The first is by water baptismal, and the second, which is commonly known as the baptism of fire (water and spirit).

The church, the ecclesia, the called out ones, who are now fully functional to operate in the kingdom of God, have the power to forgive sins, just as Jesus said to the woman caught in adultery, Go and sin no more. We as kingdom ambassadors, who are the embodiment of the church, the mobile temple of God have the authority to forgive sins. NOTE: John 20:23, "Whose soever sins ye remit, they are remitted unto them; and whose soever sins ye retain, they are retained." This is the King James version, which this book is referenced by. But let's take a look for clarity sake at the American Standard Version, "Whose soever sins ye forgive, they are forgiven unto them; whose soever sins ye retain, they are retained." The mobile church, who is walking in power and authority also have the ability to exercise the nine gifts of the Spirit. It is ashame that there are some denominations who do not believe that the gifts of the Spirit are in operation in today's church. I reiterate, they are heaven bound, but powerless in the earth realm. They are saved by the heart confession and water baptism, but void of the power of God.

When Jesus was demanded of the Pharisees when the kingdom of God would come, he said in Luke 17:21, "Neither shall they say, Lo here! Or, lo there! For behold, the kingdom of God is within you" (the treasure hidden in earthen vessels) (Christ in you, the hope of glory). In I Corinthians 4:20 the word of God says, "For the kingdom of God is not in word, but in power." This is the authority that has been given to the manifest sons of God of whom the whole earth is waiting. In Romans 8:19 it reads, "For the earnest expectation of the creature waiteth for the manifestation of the sons of God." Again, the word "sons" is in plural form, for it is not speaking of Jesus, singular, for he was the first born among many brethren. This is the Joel army that is about to be empowered to prepare a church, a bride, for the second coming of Jesus, the Christ, the son of the living God.

We will conclude this book with **Glorious Zion in the Kingdom Age**. A declaration and a decree by the prophet Isaiah, Let he who has an ear, hear this prophetic declaration. Isaiah 60, **"Arise, shine; for thy light is come, and the glory of the Lord is risen upon thee**.

For, behold, the darkness shall cover the earth, and gross darkness the people: but the Lord shall arise upon thee, and his glory shall be seen upon thee. And the Gentiles shall come to thy light, and kings to the brightness of thy rising.

Lift up thine eyes round about, and see: all they gather themselves together, they come to thee: **thy sons shall come from far, and thy daughters shall be nursed at thy side**.

Then thou shalt see, and flow together, and thine heart shall fear, and be enlarged; because the abundance of the sea shall be converted unto thee, the forces of the Gentiles shall come unto thee.

The multitude of camels shall cover thee, the dromedaries of Midian and Ephah; all they from Sheba shall come: they shall bring gold and incense; and they shall shew forth the praises of the Lord.

All the flocks of Kedar shall be gathered together unto thee, the rams of Nebaioth shall minister unto thee: they shall come up with acceptance on mine altar, and I will glorify the house of my glory.

Who are these that fly as a cloud, and as the doves to their windows?

Surely the isles shall wait for me, and the ships of Tarshish first, **to bring thy sons from afar, their silver and their gold with them,** unto the name of the Lord thy God, and to the Holy One of Israel, because he hath glorified thee.

And the sons of strangers shall build up thy walls, and their kings shall minister unto thee: for in my wrath I smote thee, but in my favour have I had mercy on thee.

Therefore thy gates shall be open continually; they shall not be shut day nor night; that men may bring unto thee the forces of the Gentiles, and that their kings may be brought.

For the nation and kingdom that will not serve thee shall perish; yea, those nations shall be utterly wasted.

The glory of Lebanon shall come unto thee, the fir tree, the pine tree, and the box together, to beautify the place of my sanctuary; and I will make the place of my feet glorious.

The sons also of them that afflicted thee shall come bending unto thee; and all they that despised thee shall bow themselves down at the soles of thy feet; and they shall call thee; The city of the Lord, The Zion of the Holy One of Israel.

Whereas thou has been forsaken and hated, so that no man went through thee, I will make thee an eternal excellency, a joy of many generations.

Thou shalt also suck the milk of the Gentiles, and shalt suck the breast of kings: and thou shalt know that I the Lord am thy Saviour and thy Redeemer, the mighty One of Jacob.

For brass I will bring gold, and for iron I will bring silver, and for wood brass, and for stones iron: I will also make thy officers peace, and thine exactors righteousness.

Violence shall no more be heard in thy land, wasting nor destruction within thy borders; but thou shalt call thy walls Salvation, and thy gates Praise.

The sun shall be no more thy light by day; neither for brightness shall the moon give light unto thee: but the Lord shall be unto thee an everlasting light, and thy God thy glory.

Thy sun shall no more go down; neither shall thy moon withdraw itself: for the Lord shall be thine everlasting light, and the days of thy mourning shall be ended.

Thy people also shall be all righteous: they shall inherit the land for ever, the branch of my planting, the work of my hands, that I may be glorified.

(22) A little one shall become a thousand, and a small one a strong nation: I the Lord will hasten it in his time."

Prophetic Instructions From the Apostle

Now I want you to read the next few verses while standing to declare and to decree into the atmosphere. Isaiah 61:1-3a, "The Spirit of the Lord God is upon me; because the Lord hath anointed me to preach good tidings unto the meek; he hath sent me to bind up the brokenhearted, to proclaim liberty to the captives, and the opening of the prison to them that are bound; To proclaim the acceptable year of the Lord, and the day of vengeance of our God; to comfort all that mourn; To appoint unto them that mourn in Zion, to give unto them beauty for ashes, the oil of joy for mourning, the garment of praise for the spirit of heaviness."

Psalms 110:1-3, "The Lord said unto my Lord, Sit thou at my right hand, until I make thine enemies thy footstool. The Lord shall send the rod of thy strength out of Zion: rule thou in the midst of thine enemies. Thy people shall be willing in the day of the power, in the beauties of holiness from the womb of the morning: thou hast the dew of thy youth."

Matthew 22:44, "The Lord said unto my Lord, Sit thou on my right hand till I make thine enemies thy footstool?"

Mark 12: 36, "For David himself said by the Holy Ghost, The Lord said to my Lord, Sit thou on my right hand, till I make thine enemies thy footstool."

Luke 20:43, "Till I make thine enemies thy footstool."

Acts 2:34-35, "For David is not ascended into the heavens: but he saith himself, The Lord said unto my Lord, Sit thou on my right hand, Until I make thy foes thy footstool."

Hebrews 1:13, "But to which on the angels said he at any time, Sit on my right hand, until I make thine enemies thy footstool?"

Hebrews 10:13, From henceforth expecting till his enemies be made his footstool."

The beginning. Back to the future. The alpha and the omega.

The Essence Of This Book

I've written this book Upon This Rock as a mandate from God to bring you, the reader, into your manifest destiny. From the eyes of an apostolic view this tapestry of historical data and revelatory insight will awaken the sleeping giant, or should I say the 21st Century Valley of Dry Bones. Through a prophetic enlightening you, the reader, will begin to understand the urgency of your calling and election. As the trumpet is being sounded throughout Zion you must run for cover (covering) to receive your Malachi 4:5 Elijah blessing. For those who are not covered already, it is imperative that you position yourself for the next move of God. This apostolic wind of the Spirit is a refreshing that is come to ignite the remnant and the elect.

In this discourse you, the reader will see and understand that God is in full control. As we take a broad look over the historical events that has led us to this present time, let us examine the Apostles of the Lamb, the scattering of the church, the fall of Saul of Tarsus, the Pauline Epistles onto Catholicism, the Prophet Martin Luther, John Huss, John Wycliffe, John Wesley, just to name a few, it is this writer's intent that there be a full disclosure of the Reformation, its pitfalls, and progression. As a wise master builder it is incumbent that we bridge the gap and paint a vivid picture with broad strokes of where we are at in the time table of God and what we must do to advance the Kingdom and prepare a bride for the second coming of Christ Jesus, who is sitting on the right-hand of God awaiting till his enemies be made his footstool. It is time for the manifest sons of God to arise and shine and take their place in eternity.

Come Lord Jesus

Apostle M.P. Sterling

Edwards Brothers Malloy
Thorofare, NJ USA
February 21, 2014